CAREERS WITH HORSES

Careers
With
Horses

Georgie Henschel

STANLEY PAUL, LONDON

Stanley Paul & Co Ltd
3 Fitzroy Square, London W1P 6JD

An imprint of the Hutchinson Publishing Group

London Melbourne Sydney Auckland
Wellington Johannesburg and agencies
throughout the world

First published 1975
© Georgie Henschel 1975
Photographs © Gerry Cranham, Keystone Press,
Leslie Lane, Press Association, Syndication International

Printed in Great Britain by The Anchor Press Ltd
and bound by Wm Brendon & Son Ltd
both of Tiptree, Essex

ISBN 0 09 124950 3 (cased)
ISBN 0 09 124951 1 (paperback)

Contents

To the memory of my father, George
Henschel, musician, lover of nature and
of horses, who shared my pleasure in
riding into his eightieth year.

Acknowledgements

Although it would not be possible for me to acknowledge all the people from whose experience during my years with horses I have benefited, I would like to express my gratitude to those who have spent time and trouble providing me with accurate information for particular sections of this book. For National Hunt training and racing, my thanks to Kenneth and Rhona Oliver; for details of Hunt service, to David Thomson, Master of the Berwickshire Hunt, and his sister Jean; and to William Elsey, Malton, for flat-racing. For the chapter on veterinary training and animal nursing I was given invaluable help by G. C. Rafferty, B.Sc., MRCVS, and by the Glasgow Veterinary College. I am grateful to R. N. Clarke, Field Officer of the Worshipful Company of Farriers, for information about farriery apprentices, and to my own farrier Donald Fraser for many practical details. And I thank Donald Wright, Saddler by Appointment, for being so informative both about the craft of saddlery and the business of being a saddler.

Lastly I thank Elwyn Hartley Edwards, editor of *Riding*, for encouraging me to start writing about horses and for allowing me to use in this book some of the material originally collected for a series of articles in his magazine.

1   What It Takes

General introduction; what type of person, what type of life entailed. There are many different types of career – but what they all entail in respect of character of careerist.

There are some careers you should only follow if you are sure enough of your choice to stick to it, in spite of tempting alternatives or adult discouragement. The stage, for example. When I was young there was a Noël Coward song called 'Don't put your daughter on the stage, Mrs Worthington', which told in graphic and intimidating, if also very funny, detail of the perils and pitfalls with which Mrs Worthington's daughter would have to cope before the day came, if it ever did, when she saw her name in lights.

A career with horses is a little similar.

Hard Work and Dedication

It's not enough to like horses, even to be passionately devoted to them, though, of course, like them you must. It's not enough to enjoy riding. Far from it. In any kind of career with horses, only a small proportion of your time will be spent actually on their backs. So if you think from watching television that it would be so glamorous to become a show-jumper: think again. The talent for show-jumping, or for any kind of riding, may be born in people, but it is hard work and dedication that brings them to the top. Nor should you think that because you have helped in the local stables at weekends, or had your own pony and ridden since you were six, that any riding establishment, or any employer, will be madly keen to pay you for your untrained services. Today, to make a successful career with horses, you must train as you would for any other career; rather more seriously than for some and probably more seriously than you may have realized. A career with horses isn't something to be entered into lightly. It is not a 'job', it's a way of life, as farming, or nursing, or being a creative artist are ways of life; a way to which you should feel yourself irresistibly drawn, and irrevocably committed. If you don't think of it in this way, don't think of it at all. There are plenty of other careers you can follow which, if you like horses, will eventually provide you with enough money to buy one for yourself, and do what you like with it, as a hobby.

Character Requirements

There are different kinds of careers with horses; it is a good thing to consider them all before you decide which training to follow. But they all require certain particular attributes of character.

Anyone working with horses, or with any animal, should be patient, intelligent, calm in emergencies, and firm and determined without being rough; not nervy, excitable or hot-tempered. And while it is natural to be ambitious, your ambition should be objective, to work towards becoming as good as possible in your particular line, rather than to aim for quick personal success to boost your own ego. You should also have a well-developed sense of responsibility towards both animals and humans. The horses you look after, when you come to work with them, will depend on you for their every need; while to their owner, your employer, they will represent a considerable financial investment. I can assure you that anyone for whom you may work during your life with horses will want above all to know that you are a responsible person, not someone who is likely to show-off on their horses when they're not about, or in any way to put your own pleasure before the welfare of your charges.

No Clock-watchers

Another vital point is that although nowadays rates of pay for all kinds of qualified horse-people are good, and, in theory, related to the hours worked, work with horses is not, and never can be, entirely regulated by the clock. If you are a confirmed clock-watcher, a career with horses is not for you. Animals, like humans, can become ill. Individual horses may at some time need extra care and attention; there will be days when things go wrong or the unexpected happens, and you can't clock out at five. The lorry may be late collecting a horse for travelling; you may be late back from a show; your hunters will undoubtedly often come in wet, dirty and tired just when you want your tea. All these things, and many more, are hazards with which you must be prepared to cope willingly and cheerfully; if you do, your employer will be only too glad to repay you with extra time off when things are slack. You should always remember, against the day when you yourself may become an employer, that the majority do a lot of 'extra time' themselves, because their horses are their lives; consequently, they haven't much use for people who only think of when they can be finished.

A further discouragement is that it isn't always summer! While you may enjoy stable work in fine weather – mucking out, sweeping the yard, keeping a tidy manure heap, carrying bales and filling hay-nets and all the rest of it – how will you feel about doing these things in the wet, cold, frost, and perhaps snow, of winter? And exercising, so pleasant when the day is nice, how about those cold, dark mornings or dreary, damp afternoons? And how about possibly having to spend time and energy laying a straw ring for the horses to work on when the ground is iron hard? Not every one has an indoor school; even then, you may have to help keep the surface raked and clean.

Physical Work

Which brings me to the physical side of a career with horses. Unless you become a really high-powered instructor, or make so much money you can employ a lot of help, more or less any kind of horsey career will entail a certain amount of fairly hard physical work. This doesn't mean you have to be big, brawny and bulging with muscle, only that you should be reasonably healthy. The work itself will build up the muscle! What you do need, more than physical strength or toughness, is a certain strength of character. The ability to stay on an even keel: not to let things get you down, so that you don't take it out on the horse when he stands on your foot (as they all do sooner or later), or burst into tears if your riding teacher in a fit of desperation shouts at you, or fall into despair because in a few months you haven't been able to turn yourself into Princess Anne or Lester Piggott. In learning anything, there always comes a moment when everything seems hopeless and you might as well give up. That's usually the turning point. Get over it, work through it, and suddenly, difficulties will begin to resolve themselves and you'll see success ahead.

Variety of Careers

Now for some encouragement. There is such a variety of careers to choose from, that if you're determined to work with horses, there's sure to be one which particularly appeals to you.

If you have a strong personality, get on well with people, and feel you may have a gift for teaching, you can train to become an Instructor, progressing through the British Horse Society's graded examinations. If you like riding and looking after horses better than coping with people, and the idea of teaching alarms you, you can become a qualified groom, later a Stable Manager – again, through the British Horse Society's exams. Or you can gain the Groom's Diploma of the Association of British Riding Schools. If you are mad about racing you can become an apprentice in a flat-racing stable, and perhaps one day a jockey. For this, however, you shouldn't be too big, although you can now be a girl; until 1975 all apprentices were male. If you are a bit big, or if you want to jump as well as race, you can go into National Hunt Stables. In either, if you don't make the grade as a jockey you can have a good future, starting as a well-paid 'lad', or 'lass'. Or, you can work in Hunt stables, with the aim of becoming a professional huntsman. If you are specially interested in the theories and principles of breeding and the handling and training of young stock you can train for a career in stud work, qualifying through the National Pony Society's examinations. This is a most rewarding career, and one in which trained people can always be sure of finding good positions.

Nursing Auxiliaries

There is also the veterinary profession. As with human medicine, you have first to qualify in general veterinary surgery and medicine. Later, there will be opportunities for you to specialize in horses. Or you can train to become a RANA, a Registered Animal Nursing Auxiliary, a fairly new, and expanding, subsidiary to the veterinary profession.

Then there are two other professions, both vital to the

horse world, neither of which may have occurred to you but which both offer the chance of interesting and lucrative careers: farriery and saddlery.

So you see, whether you're a boy or a girl, there's a fairly wide choice. Remember, though, that if you rise to the top of your profession, as naturally you hope to do, and perhaps start a business of your own, the more you know about the business side of things beforehand, the better. If, therefore, before your training, or perhaps during it, you can also learn typing, and something about book-keeping and the costing of a business, it will be to your advantage. Other advantages are a good knowledge of your own language, and a fairly wide general knowledge. Your training is bound to be specialized and specialization is a good thing, but it can be overdone. There are some very dull people who can only think and talk about their own subject. So, keep your mind wide open. Listen to knowledgeable people when you get the chance, learn to be a good mixer, and a good conversationalist – and read. Innumerable books have been written about every kind of horsey activity, and though you, or your teacher, may not agree with everything a writer says, you will get something from each one. Try also to develop an 'eye for a horse'. When you go to shows, don't just watch the jumping, watch the showing classes too. What makes a good horse or pony? Would you have assessed them in the same way as the judge had done? And if you do watch the jumping, don't just sit spellbound with your mouth open. Why did that horse refuse, and this one go clear? The horse or the rider? Why are some riders more pleasing to watch than others?

You will find that anything and everything that broadens not only your horsey outlook, but your outlook on life, will help you in whatever line in which you decide to specialize.

2   Teaching and Stable Management Examinations

The British Horse Society's examinations; what they are; what they qualify one for; how one takes them. The Association of British Riding Schools' Groom's Diploma.

If you want to teach riding or perhaps one day to have your own riding school, you will need to qualify to do so by taking one, two, or more of the British Horse Society's examinations. Other groups and societies award diplomas and certificates that are valid for other kinds of horse activity, but it is only the British Horse Society's certificates that will qualify you to teach. The reason for this is that, under the British Equestrian Federation, the Society is the recognized body responsible, in Britain, for setting and maintaining standards of both riding and teaching. Because of its official standing, and the fact that it offers examinations as stepping-stones to worth-while careers, many County Education Authorities are prepared to give grants to people wishing to take them.

The Examinations

The four examinations are: the Assistant Instructor's, which you can take when you are seventeen and a half; the Intermediate Instructor's the Instructor's, for which you must be twenty-two; and the Fellowship, which is a very advanced examination indeed, achieved by only the most talented riders and the most gifted teachers.

Because it takes intelligence to become a good instructor,

you have to have certain academic qualifications before enrolling on a course. As from the 1st of January 1976, you will need four 'O' levels, or four CSE Grade I passes; that is, unless you are already twenty or over, when the Society considers your extra maturity may make up for your possible lack of scholastic achievement. There was a time when you had to have a First Aid Certificate, but as it was often difficult for candidates to train for these, from now on you will only be expected to have a good common-sensical knowledge of what to do in case of an accident and you will be asked questions to prove your knowledge.

The Assistant Instructor

Now, before going into details of the syllabus of the course and how to train to become, first, an Assistant Instructor, I think you should fully understand that the idea behind these examinations is not just to produce good riders. Naturally, as you progress, your riding will improve; but the Society's object in offering them is not only for you to improve your own standards, it is to produce a large body of trained instructors capable of handing on the precepts of correct riding to the ever growing number of people who yearly take up riding and horse owning. So you shouldn't sit for these examinations because you think it will look smart to have certain letters after your name, nor do you want to think of them as a sort of status symbol Mary Jane has her 'AI', so why not I? Even if you only train for and pass the *first* of the examinations, I think it is your duty to make use of your training, and teach, not to sit back and admire yourself for your success!

　　Maybe you don't know if you want to teach, or even if you could. Well, fair enough, but take a look at your attitude to riding. If you are riding with friends, or, if you don't ride yet, if you are watching others; do you ever feel they don't look quite right, and you would like to tell them something that might help them? Do you watch even 'the great', live or on television, with a critical as well as an admiring eye? If so, you probably have the gift of teaching somewhere inside you, because I am sure that becoming a good teacher of riding is very largely a matter of having a 'good eye', of being able to assess the picture a horse and rider make as a partnership; if the picture is not quite right, of being able to see how to correct it. Riding, after all, is a plastic art; the greatest riders, and the greatest teachers of riding, are in their own way artists. As in all arts, you have to learn the technicalities; you cannot teach anything until you have a sound understanding of the subject. But how successfully you can put this teaching across to different ages and stages of riders is a matter of talent and temperament. If you are a shy person, for instance, I think you would find teaching adults a strain, though you might be very successful with children. Not that you need to be brash, or hard-boiled; only that to inspire confidence in pupils, you must have confidence in yourself, and in your ability, while teaching, to hold their attention and concentration. Which, I may say, takes a great deal of concentration on your part.

I have sometimes been able to watch Assistant Instructor examinations, and have always been specially interested in the teaching part, seeing how candidates get down to the job of trying to give a lesson. Naturally, it is a bit alarming to have to do your stuff in front of a panel of examiners, so it's not surprising that most give the impression of being so overawed by the occasion that all they can do is, quite obviously, repeat things their instructors have said to them. Encouragingly, though, there have also been the odd few with talent and enthusiasm, who, the moment they started their lesson, became so engrossed that they forgot all about the examiners and actually managed in ten minutes concentrated work to improve the riding of each one of their long-suffering 'guinea-pigs'.

B

Educational Grants

I said at the beginning that you may be able to get a Further Education grant to train for the Assistant Instructor's examination. I am afraid the operative word is 'may'; not all Authorities have accepted the fact that a career with horses is to be taken as seriously as any other. The only way you can find this out is by making representations to your own local Authority. You should do this, if you're still at school, by discussing the matter with your headmaster or headmistress, who will make the initial approach to the chief education officer of your county. If the county has already made similar grants, there will be no difficulty. If not, you will have to do a bit of pressurizing, and you can also contact the Training and Development Officer of the British Horse Society, who is only too glad to try to help people get grants from Authorities who may never have heard of such things as careers with horses. If you have trouble, write to the Training & Development Office, British Horse Society, National Equestrian Centre, Kenilworth, Warwickshire, CV8 2LR. If you are older, have already left school and wish to train, you can sometimes get financial help if you contact the Training Opportunities Scheme of the Department of Employment.

The reason for obtaining a further education grant is that for a horse career, as for any other, you have to spend time and money training to qualify, for although the syllabus of the 'AI' exam is not a particularly difficult one, I don't think anyone under twenty, however experienced, could possibly pass without having taken a course of instruction. Don't be entirely put off, however, if you cannot get a grant; there are various ways of taking your training, some more economical than others.

When I say the syllabus of the exam is not particularly

difficult, I mean it in the sense that the knowledge expected of you is really only the basic knowledge any responsible person employing you would expect you to have. This is, however, perhaps wider than you may have realized, especially concerning horse care and stable management.

The Four Exam Sections

The examination is divided into four parts: Equitation, Stable Management and Horsemastership, Minor Ailments, and Instructional Ability. To pass, you must not only satisfy the examiners in each section, you must more than satisfy them in one at least, because the total of marks they give you must come to seventy-five per cent of the whole. If, however, you fail only the Instructional part, and pass the others well, you can gain thereby the Certificate of Horsemastership.

To pass in Equitation, you must be a competent, correct rider, able to jump fences up to one metre, to ride without your stirrups, and to be effective on different types and temperaments of horses: during exam you will probably ride about six different ones. Stable Management and Horsemastership covers a wide range of subjects, from the general routine of a yard through grooming, rugging, bandaging, trimming, plaiting, to the feeding and care generally of horses both stabled and at grass. Minor Ailments is a written paper; you will be allowed forty-five minutes to answer five questions out of eight. During Intructional Ability tests, you will be expected to show not only that you know what to teach, but that you can control your ride, using your voice so that your ride can hear you (more important than you think), and demonstrate to your pupils when necessary. The cost of taking the examination is £12·50 (1975); if you pass, you are entitled to put the letters BHSAI after your name, and you will find no difficulty whatsoever in getting a good, well-paid position. You should remember, however, that this is only the first rung of the ladder. Whatever employment you do take after qualifying, you should do your best to work and study for the next rungs – the Intermediate and the full Instructor's exams, each of which if you pass will considerably increase your earning power and widen your scope. Apart from stud work, which is highly specialized, practically any position in the horse world of any country is open to a BHS Instructor, or to a Fellow of the Society. Also, as you are now qualified to teach more advanced and competitive pupils as well as to train students for the 'AI', good riding training establishments will fall over themselves to employ you.

Training

The usual way of training for the Assistant Instructor's exam is to go to a reputable riding training establishment, which will probably be owned by a BHS Instructor or Fellow of the Society, or where the Chief Instructor is sure to be one or the other. You can go either as a working pupil or as a student. As a working pupil, you will be expected to pay for your board and lodging, but you will pay no fees for your instruction, you will repay that in work. You will also be expected to stay for a minimum period, generally one year. You will live either in the owner's house or in a cottage, flat or caravan which you will share with other students; or you may have to live in digs in the nearby town or village. The cost will vary between £7 and £10 per week (1975). It is just possible that if you are a very talented rider and have a fair experience of stable work you may be taken on for nothing, but don't count on this.

You can train as a fee-paying student. If you are experienced, perhaps have your own horse or pony and belong to the Pony Club, and have passed your 'B' test, you may be able to train to exam standard in a three-, or six-, month course; perhaps even less. Whether you can train in this way depends, of course, upon whether your parents can afford it. If you do, and have your own horse or pony, there are establishments which will let you bring it, although you will have to pay for its keep. A relatively short exam-training course, which will probably be residential unless you actually live next door to the school, can cost about £35 a week (1975).

Choosing a Training School

Having decided how you want to train and what you can afford, the choice of where to go is important. There are many good training establishments; by writing to the British Horse Society, you can obtain a list of those the Society recognizes and recommends. Decide from the list which you would like to go to; write to the Principal, and ask for the prospectus or brochure; ask also if you may go to see them, and if there would be a vacancy for you at the time you want to start your training. The establishment will in return wish to see you ride; some like you to spend a few days, even a week, with them, so that they can assess your capabilities and potentialities, and thereby get an idea of the time it may take for you to reach the necessary standard. If you can decide where you want to train before applying for your grant, it will be helpful, because costs and charges do vary from one to another. What I think is most important when choosing your place of training, is that you should feel at home and at ease in its atmosphere. Some are large, with up to thirty or more students. If you are gregarious, you will enjoy that. Some are much smaller, concentrating on perhaps no more than two or three pupils at a time. You may feel this is more your cup of tea; but remember, the fewer there are of you, the more you must be prepared to make the cffort to get on with your fellow trainees. Find out how much actual riding instruction you are going to get. Roughly speaking, working pupils can expect an hour a day, paying students will probably get two riding sessions. Find out who gives the lessons. Assistant Instructors will probably give you some; some will also be given, especially as you progress, by a more advanced Instructor.

However you take your training, you will have to work. Your day, if you are a working pupil, may start at 7 a.m.; you will have two, three or even four horses to 'do'; that is, muck out, groom, feed, and generally look after. You will probably have a riding lesson in the morning, in the afternoon, maybe a teaching one, or you will watch others being taught, or learn how to lunge, or be yourself lunged on a horse, or listen to lectures. And of course you will have to clean tack, wash out buckets, help keep the place clean and tidy, fill hay-nets, fulfil all the ordinary duties of a stable yard. You will probably finish about 5 p.m., though actual routine varies from place to place. But make no mistake – there will be plenty of work to keep your body exercised, as well as plenty to learn to keep your mind active.

Private Training

There are other ways of training. For instance, a knowledgeable private owner may be glad to teach you, keep you and perhaps pay you a little pocket money in return for your help. Even so, to pass the exam, you will need a short official course before taking it, because however good your teacher may be, he or she may not know exactly what the examiners want. Also, if they have no indoor school, you will have to get used to working in one before exam day.

Last, but by no means least, there are in this country excellent training centres run by Instructors who are outside the Establishment, which train riders and horses to exceptionally high standards. Although he has now retired, Captain Edy Goldman's Cheshire Equestrian Training Centre was particularly successful. The number of accomplished riders who have been trained by, or have had help from, Captain Goldman is legion. One of his pupils, has already made equestrian history: Sheila Willcox, the only person to have won Badminton three times running, and now, nearly twenty years later, the only woman to have been asked to train an Olympic Three Day Event team: Canada's for 1976.

All the same, on the principle that if a motorist wants to take his driving test he must have at least a few lessons from an official instructor to learn how to pass it, so must you, if you want to take a BHS examination. No matter how advanced your riding may be, have at least a few lessons from an official instructor who can teach you what the Society's examiners will expect you to know. Remember that in today's highly competitive world, unless you are abnormally talented or abnormally rich, it is an advantage in any career to possess the qualifications accepted by the Establishment.

Until 1974 the two steps up to full BHS teaching qualifications were the Assistant Instructor's and the Instructor's examinations. From 1975 on, the Society has decided to bridge the rather large gap between these two with an intermediate one: an examination which will be called the Intermediate Instructor's. To take this exam, you will have to have passed your 'AI', and it will be a considerably more searching test of your genuine ability to teach. You will not only have to take a ride of some four to six pupils, as you do for the 'AI', but you'll be expected to be able to prepare pupils for the 'AI', or for Pony Club 'B' test, or Riding Club exam Stage III. You'll have to be able to coach over show-jumps and cross-country fences, to Pony Club or Riding Club Horse

Trials standard; and to teach up to Elementary dressage. Moreover, you must know how to lunge, and will be asked to give a lesson on the lunge to a genuine novice rider. And you'll have to give a short talk, on general stable management and routine, as you might do to a group of pupils preparing for their 'AI'.

As from October 1976, if you want to take the Instructor's exam, you'll have to have passed the Intermediate Instructor's one first.

You can get the syllabus for all the BHS examinations, from the National Equestrian Centre, Stoneleigh, Kenilworth, Warwicks, CV8 2LR; address your letter to the Training and Development Office, British Horse Society.

BHS Horsemastership Examinations

It will delight you to know that the British Horse Society does also offer career examinations for people who may not want to teach: those who want to qualify as good riders and stable managers, but who shudder at the thought of having to go through the motions of telling others how to ride.

The two non-teaching examinations are the Certificate of Horsemastership, which used to be called rather more simply the Horsemaster's Certificate, and the Stable Manager's Certificate. The first is very easily explained, because it is exactly the same as the Assistant Instructor's, but without the teaching, and you have to be seventeen and a half before you take it. However, you don't need any special academic qualifications, and it costs less – £10 instead of £12·50 (1975). The Society has also left a loophole in case, after passing it, you decide that you do want to teach. Provided you do so after three months and within three years of passing the Horsemastership, you can take the teaching section of the Assistant Instructor's examination on its own. I think this is very sensible. Of course, you may be quite sure now that you don't want to teach but once you get out into the horse world and see the low standards of riding that still prevail here and there you may find yourself inspired to do so. Naturally, if you did this, you would have to have the necessary 'O' levels or Grade I passes, unless by then you were over twenty.

The Stable Manager

The Stable Manager's examination is very comprehensive. Anyone passing it will be fully capable of taking responsibility for the running and management of any kind of yard, or of owning and running their own, and training student grooms. If you wanted your establishment to be an actual riding school, however, you would have to employ someone qualified as an instructor to do the teaching. The standard of riding expected from candidates for this examination is high, but you don't have to know how to tell others how to do it. The examination also calls for a knowledge of all the things that go to make up the business side of horse and stable management.

Groom's Diploma, Association of British Riding Schools

If the British Horse Society is the body officially representative of all the interests and aspects of the horse world, the Association of British Riding Schools is the one representing the particular interests of professional riding school proprietors and riding masters. As such, its main objects are to raise and maintain the standards of professional schools; not only of the instruction given, but of the condition of riding school animals, and to ensure the competence of the grooms employed to look after them.

It is not so easy as you might think for the professional riding school, busy with the day-to-day routine of lessons, hacking and exercising liveries, to find competent grooms capable of looking after and turning horses out properly, as well as being responsible enough to accompany riders out hacking, perhaps even hunting. Newly qualified 'AIs' are unlikely to be mature enough; besides, many of them want to take up work where they can continue their training towards becoming Instructors. The ABRS has therefor devised an examination of its own, the Groom's Diploma. This examination is almost entirely practical. The examiners want to be assured that you not only know the theory of horse and stable management, but that you can actually perform all the necessary duties. If you gain this Diploma, it is a guarantee to employers that you have the physical as well as the mental ability to be an efficient groom. There are only two qualifications for taking it: you must be seventeen and a half years old, and you must have had at least eighteen months of full-time occupation with horses.

This means that immediately on leaving school you can try to find a riding school or a livery stable which will take you on, perhaps for a small wage in return for your work, and at the same time give you the necessary grounding in stable duties and routine, and in riding experience. Certain riding schools which are members of the Association specifically offer training for the Diploma; but all good ones, if you can get into them, will be able to give you enough training and experience for you to try for it at the end of eighteen months. The cost is £7 (1975). If you write to the Secretary of the Association of British Riding Schools, Chesham House, 56 Green End Road, Sawtry, Huntingdon, you will be able to get precise details of where and when examinations for the Diploma are being held in any particular year, and a list of Riding Schools which would be willing to help you take it.

This is a very worth-while qualification to possess, particularly for those of you who don't so much want to specialize as to have an interesting and varied life with horses, either in this country or abroad. Like the BHS certificates, most countries recognize the ABRS Diploma as being a warranty of competence.

The Starting Age

It is very sensible that all these examinations should have a minimum starting age: seventeen and a half for the BHSAI, the Horsemastership and the ABRS Groom's Diploma; twenty-two for the BHS Instructor's, and twenty-five for the Fellowship. Equally sensibly, however, they haven't a maximum age limit! You don't have to start your climb up the ladder the moment you leave school; in fact, it is a good idea to have a second string to your bow, and take a secretarial or short business course before your training. Also, I do know there are lots of people over twenty who suddenly get sick of their routine office jobs, in towns or cities, and wonder if by then they are too old to set out on a career with horses. Certainly not if they're active, outdoor people. In fact, provided they have the necessary talent, they may make better professionals, because they will have had time seriously to weigh up the pros and cons of a life with horses.

Finally, don't think that because there are a number of unqualified people working successfully in the contemporary horse world, you don't really need to bother to qualify yourself. Most of those people started their careers before the days of examinations, before the formation of the British Horse Society, perhaps even before that of its predecessor, the Institute of the Horse. They have built their reputations on merit, and have become qualified through long experience. I cannot say too often or too forcefully that in the horse world, while examinations are a necessary means of setting and assessing standards, what really counts is experience.

By the way, don't think these examinations, particularly the BHS Instructors', are for girls only. Any young man who is a talented rider and feels he might like to instruct can qualify. It is only fairly recently that there have come to be so many more female than male riding teachers. Before the last war, the best riding instructors were nearly always men, who had qualified through training at the cavalry training schools of their particular countries. To-day the famous French Cavalry School at Saumur is one of the few of these still in existence. In this country the male riding teachers of the future must qualify through the same BHS examinations as their female counterparts, and I hope many will do so. Apart from the fact that there will always be good and highly paid openings for really talented male instructors; human nature being what it is, there will always be some women who prefer to be taught by men, just as there will always be some men who will take instruction better from a woman!

3 Training for Stud Work

The National Pony Society examinations for stud work. What they are; how and where to take them; what they qualify one for. A note on training generally for stud work – for males, courses in bloodstock breeding, etc.

If I were young again and starting on my life with horses I know the career I would choose; I would train for the National Pony Society's Diploma in stud work. For lots of reasons, some of which I think may appeal to many of you.

Firstly, stud work, which, as well as breeding, includes the handling, breaking and schooling of young animals, is the basis on which every other horse activity rests. If there were no stallions, no brood mares, no matings and no foals, there would be no successive generations of horses and ponies for us to ride, show, hunt, jump, and generally enjoy. That's obvious. What may not be so obvious is that it is the handling, breaking and schooling which make or mar the thousands of horse and pony foals born each year. Far too many are spoilt by ignorant training, or no proper training, for the simple reason that although there are many knowledgeable breeders in the horse world of today, there are far too few knowledgeable handlers and breakers: what in the old days would have been called 'nagsmen'. I firmly believe that no foal is born vicious or a rogue; it is incorrect human handling – sometimes brutal, sometimes over-sentimental – which produces warped equine temperaments.

A Field of Opportunity

Secondly, because there are relatively few trained stud workers, compared with 'AIs', once qualified you can be sure of constant, well-paid employment. Moreover, if you become particularly good at breaking and schooling, you can, as time goes on, set yourself up professionally to break, school and produce other people's young horses.

The third reason goes rather deeper and touches what could be called the ethics of breeding. I believe that if more people thought seriously about breeding itself, and the responsibilities it imposes, or should impose, on them, there might be less indiscriminate breeding and fewer foals might be born; so many, after their initial cuddly and fluffy stage to become unwanted.

I believe we humans should never forget that although it is the mare who carries and produces the foal, it is we who decided she should conceive. Dogs and cats are so different. They can please themselves and surprise us by producing litters, nor do they seem to miss the ones we have to destroy if we're not to become overrun by dogs and cats. Horses are very seldom free to breed to their own desires. If we send our mare to the stallion of our choice it is we who must take the responsibility for the foal she produces.

Until you have seen a foal born you will probably never quite understand this. It struck me forcibly sixteen years ago, as I watched my first brood mare lick her curly, still wet, newly born filly. But for me the little filly would never have been born; more than that, her dam would never have known the deep maternal satisfaction of licking her dry, nuzzling her towards her full udder, and standing over her in drowsy and proud content when, replete, she collapsed back on to the straw. Many of my mares have had foals since then, but I have never lost the feeling that for all of them, it is I who am ultimately responsible.

Learning to Live with Horses

The best way we can do this is to learn how to handle, train and educate young horses and ponies so that they mature into sensible, good-tempered, well-mannered adults; as such they'll be far more likely to be well treated all their lives than if they grow up scatty, nervous and suspicious through bad handling and bad, or too early, breaking.

A training in stud work will teach us these things. It will also teach us a great deal about the true nature of the horse as an animal; the instinct and behaviour patterns of the species *Equus caballus*, because today it tends to be only the breeding stock which has the chance to spend time at liberty and to behave naturally. The majority of domesticated horses are kept in conditions which, however excellent, are unnatural to them. Horses, by nature, are gregarious herbivores, which means that they live in herds and eat grass or whatever vegetation they can find, more or less all the time, having the kind of digestive system that needs to have an intake of food fairly constantly. So, although horses obviously come to enjoy living in the comfort of their twelve by twelves; to relish their oats and to stand for hours contentedly pulling at their hay-nets; we have taught them this against their instinct.

The behaviour patterns of horses amongst themselves are fascinating to watch; sometimes amusing, always enlightening, but they can only be observed when the horses are grazing at liberty, which, incidentally, all should be allowed to do from time to time. The more you observe and the more you get to know about the basic characteristics of horses in general by working with them at all ages and stages, the better equipped you will be to educate any particular individual young horse. So, how does one start training for stud work?

Stud Examinations

The National Pony Society's examinations are, like those of the British Horse Society, progressive. There are two of them: the Stud Assistant's Certificate and the full Diploma. The first, you can take any time after the age of sixteen, though I doubt if anyone so young could have had enough experience. For the second, you must be over twenty-one. Neither call for any specific academic qualifications, but personally I think you should have at least an 'O' level, or the equivalent, in English. Particularly if you want to go on to the full Diploma. It would be awkward if one day you wanted to start your own stud, and perhaps train students, and you found you hadn't a really good command of your own language.

With or Without Riding

Both examinations can be taken with or without riding. Naturally, to qualify without riding would slightly limit your opportunities; on the other hand, a great deal of stud work is done 'on the ground', just as a great deal of showing is done in hand. So, if you are not a particularly experienced or keen rider, but are particularly good with animals, don't be discouraged; train for the other parts of these very comprehensive examinations. If you pass, breeders and stud owners will be just as eager to employ you. You see, the standard of riding asked for is fairly high; it has to be, if you are to be capable of backing young animals and giving them correct basic schooling. But then these exams call for a high standard throughout. To pass the Certificate you have to get 70 per cent in each subject, and to gain the full Diploma, 80 per cent.

The subjects are comprehensive. Naturally there is the handling, care and management of stallions; the management and the serving of brood mares; the care, feeding and weaning of foals; and the handling of young stock and their early training which includes leading, lungeing and finally backing them. There is also a section on showing – how to prepare animals for showing and how to present different breeds and types in the ring, both adults and youngsters. You also have to know something about 'minor ailments', in particular those ailments to which breeding stock may be most liable. When it comes to riding, you must not only know, and be able to use, the correct aids, but be capable of teaching them to the horse. Your temperament comes into this, for giving young horses their first lessons calls for an extra allowance of patience allied to firmness.

Stud Training

Altogether, however much you may already know, I think you will agree that to cope with all this, you will need to go to a reputable stud and train. In fact, the syllabus of the Certificate clearly says that candidates should have had at least one year's experience on a stud before attempting it. This may sound a long time, when it is quite possible for fairly experienced people to train for the 'AI' examination in far less. On the other hand, stud work is so very different that it really does take a full year to cover all the various activities and all the stages of the mare's breeding cycle; from service to foaling to subsequent service takes just about the twelve months.

As to where you can train, if you write to the National Pony Society, 85 Cliddesden Road, Basingstoke, Hants, the Secretary will send you, as well as information about the exams, a list of the studs which accept trainees, and which the Society recommends. There aren't so many of these, but those there are are well spread out over Britain – from Cumbria to Cornwall, with two in Scotland and one in Wales. You may be able to find one not too far

c

away from where you live; you can then contact whoever owns or runs it, go to see them, and discuss your training with them. There is a possibility you may be able to get a Further Education grant for this training; again, this will depend on the attitude of your local Education Authorities towards careers with horses. When you discuss this possibility with your headmaster or headmistress make it quite clear that you want to train for *stud* work, and that so far the National Pony Society examinations are the only ones officially to qualify you to do so. Incidentally, don't think that passing them means you will only be able to work with ponies. Stud work remains the same in principle, whatever the size of the animal involved.

When you study the list of studs where you can train you will find that not all of them undertake to teach riding as well as stud work. If you want to take the riding part of the exam, and the stud you really want to go to is non-riding, don't let that put you off. You can either take an instructional riding course before you go, which if you get a grant will count as part of your training; or, if there is a good riding school anywhere near the stud, you can probably arrange to have lessons there on your days off, while you're training. In fact, if you are a reasonably good rider, certainly if you're a member of the Pony Club and have your 'B' test, what you will learn about the handling and training of young horses on the ground should enable you to understand the principles of how to ride them. Probably a short course concentrating on the riding of young horses would be enough to get you to exam standard.

Good Prospects

A point that may not have occurred to you is that if you are a very small person, but don't want to be a jockey, stud work offers you specially good prospects. Breeders of small Mountain and Moorland ponies and children's riding ponies under 13.2 hands, find it extremely difficult to get adults light enough and small enough to break and school them. However good children may be, they almost inevitably grow too big and heavy, whereas ordinary-sized adults are not only too heavy but their legs are too long! If you are about five foot tall, you could be invaluable to breeders of small ponies, because you could school ones of twelve hands and even less, with little more than the weight of a child, but the skill and intelligence of an adult.

If you are a young man, interested in stud work, the word 'pony' attached to these qualifying examinations may have made you think they're not for you. In a sense you are right, because most NPS trainees do seem to be girls. But if you don't mind spending up to a year as possibly the only male amongst a gaggle of girls, by all means, train for them; as I have explained, they qualify you for *stud* work, not simply to work on pony stud.

Bloodstock Breeding

On the other hand, I suspect that what might interest you most is the possibility of working in Thoroughbred studs – bloodstock breeding. If this is so, then you should write to the Thoroughbred Breeders' Association, 42 Portman Square, London W1; the Secretary will advise you which studs might be willing to accept you as a student, and on what terms. This is particularly suitable for young men, because although girls and women work side by side on equal terms with men and boys in racing stables, when it comes to Thoroughbred stud work men are preferred, not necessarily for all work, but certainly for everything that has to do with stallion care and handling. There is a big difference between handling and caring for a Thoroughbred stallion and handling a stallion of any other breed, not so much because of his temperament but because he is a commercial proposition, representing an investment of anything up to a million pounds. If you are a girl and do want to get into the Thoroughbred stud world I suggest you take your full NPS Diploma first; this will prove to stud owners and managers that you have enough practical experience to be let loose amongst their valuable charges.

When you gain your NPS Certificate and take your first job do try to ensure that you will be working under a good stud groom or a knowledgeable stud owner. As you work with them, you will be learning all the time, so that almost without realizing it, you will reach Diploma standard. Finally, when you are fully qualified, there will still be opportunities for you to add to your knowledge and improve your prospects. Many of the individual Breed Societies run special courses for breeders and stud workers; so does the Equine Research Station of the Animal Health Trust, at Balaton Lodge, Newmarket.

A final word to young men. If you don't manage to get into a Thoroughbred stud, don't think it is beneath your dignity to work in a 'pony' stud. However good women and girls are, there will always be some things men can do better. I've yet to see the woman who can show a Welsh cob or a Welsh Mountain stallion – or any stallion for that matter – as well as a man; not because she can't *handle* the stallion, but quite simply because she cannot run fast enough! A great many men manage highly successful pony studs; some on their own, some as one half of a married working partnership.

4   National Hunt Stables and Hunt Service

Careers in National Hunt and Hunt Stables. What these are; how one starts; what they may lead to, possibly a career as groom or Head Groom in private hunting or point-to-point stables, etc.

National Hunt

If it does seem to be mostly girls who take up certain careers with horses, there are nevertheless some which are still almost entirely male preserves. One is the National Hunt world; another is Hunt Service. If you are a young man who is not looking forward to leaving school and spending your life in some sedentary job indoors; if you like horses and an outdoor life and would rather be happy and healthy than rich with ulcers; one or the other might appeal to you. Both are professional in the fullest sense; they are not for the dilettante who thinks it might be nice to take some training and acquire a set of letters after his name. Both have the advantage that you can start on leaving school, without any previous experience at the bottom; of the ladder of course, but with pay. Neither will bring you in as much money as you might make in business or industry, or even in the coal mines; but both, as you grow older and gain experience, nearly always offer *accommodation* with the more responsible positions. This is worth consideration, for with the house there are usually also quite a few 'perks' and in these days of rising costs and rising taxation a free house and free heating and lighting are worth rather more than the equivalent amount of money in your pocket. Whether or not you do climb up the ladder will depend, naturally, on your ability and your dedication to the work.

The 'Chase Jockey

The National Hunt world is the world of steeplechasing and hurdling. The profession of National Hunt race-riding is a tough one, which calls not only for top-class horsemanship, but for an extra large allowance of 'nerve'; it may be exciting and rewarding, but it is always hazardous. A National Hunt jockey during his career will probably break most of the breakable bones in his body, yet such is his enthusiasm for the exhilarating game of riding good horses fast over fences that he'll be racing again after a fall which would have put lesser mortals out of the saddle for days, if not weeks. And not only because he probably needs the money for the ride; there are many first-class amateur steeplechase riders who have no reason other than their own enthusiasm to go on risking their necks. It is a man's game; not simply because women are not as yet permitted to ride in National Hunt races, but because it does call for a particularly masculine kind of toughness. It also calls for brains. You can't ride a race like, for example, the Grand National by just charging blindly full speed ahead, and taking or not taking every fence as it comes. You've got to think your way round, both beforehand and when you're riding, and use your imagination. What's the other fellow going to do? Or that loose horse? And a sympathetic 'feel' for the way your own horse is going, remembering that great jumping horses, if you happen to be on one, are as individual in their characters and temperaments as great human athletes.

Well, obviously not everyone who goes into the National Hunt world is going to make a top-class steeplechase jockey. But there are many other interesting activities open to you if you start by going to work in a National Hunt stable, where steeplechasers and hurdlers are trained. Very often, the trainers who run these stables are men who have retired after being successful National Hunt riders; they may, however, be women, for although women cannot be National Hunt jockeys, they can hold trainers' licences, and as such are on an equal footing with men.

Stable Lad

You can go straight from school to a National Hunt stable as a 'lad', and as such would immediately be paid at least whatever happened at the time to be the minimum agricultural wage. For the first few weeks your work would consist mostly of following one of the experienced lads round, working under his supervision until he thought you were capable of 'doing' your own two or three horses, that being the average number a lad does in most stables.

'Doing' a horse means that you look after it entirely; mucking out, bedding down, cleaning its tack, exercising, and eventually, if you become good enough, riding it out to 'work'. You would also give it its feeds, but those would be made up for you by the Head Lad or perhaps by the trainer himself. At first, if you want to ride (not all lads do), you would be taken out to exercise a quiet, reliable animal, of which there are always a few in a stable, to give new lads experience; you would be helped with your riding, you wouldn't be expected to be able to cope straight away with a fit horse in training. In many stables the lads choose which horses they want to 'do', the senior lad having first choice; everyone 'does' best on the horses they specially like. On the other hand, unless they are landed with really difficult ones, most lads tend to become almost jealously possessive of their particular charges and intensely interested in their performances on the racecourse.

Hours of Work

Your day would start at 7 a.m. or thereabouts, with feeding, mucking out, quartering and first exercise. Half an
hour for breakfast at about 9 a.m.; then more exercise and
general stable work till dinner. Afternoon work depends
on each individual trainer's routine. Some give a long
midday break, from 12 noon till 2 p.m., with thorough
grooming in the afternoon, then bedding down, feeding,
and finishing by 5 p.m. Others give the long break later,
perhaps 2 p.m. till 4 p.m., and finish later. If there are late
stables, lads take them in turns. Rather than having one day
off each week, you would probably have full weekends in
rotation, again this depends on the size of the stable and
the number of lads employed. How you live varies from
stable to stable. It may be in a hostel with a housekeeper to
cook and clean and do your washing and generally look after
you; or in a cottage with other lads, looked after by the
wife of one of the married men, or perhaps in digs nearby.
In every case a portion of your wage, about a third, will be
deducted for your board and lodging. This portion is not
subject to income tax, and as it is providing you with
everything you need, the money you do get is all 'in
your pocket'. Moreover, even as a lad, you come in for
some 'perks': a share of the trainer's bonuses for winners,
and if one of the horses you 'do' happens to be the winner,
perhaps another bonus from its delighted owner.

The Alternatives

Starting as a lad, you can get on in the National Hunt
world in two different ways: by riding, or by doing stable
work. If you do seem to have special riding ability, your
trainer will notice this, and probably give you a chance to
ride in some of the 'opportunity races' specially organized
for aspiring National Hunt stable lads. If you make good

A well-kept yard not only makes for happy, contented horses, but creates a good impression.

A National Hunt Yard and (*below*) two well-turned-out students at a Riding Training Establishment.

Riding school instruction in progress.
(*Below*) The author lungeing a young pony (lunge rein on back D of head collar).

Opposite: Racehorses at the finish of a training gallop, watched by their trainer.
(*Below*) Brooke Sanders, champion Lady Jockey of 1974. Since 1975, lady riders can apply for professional licences, and ride against men.

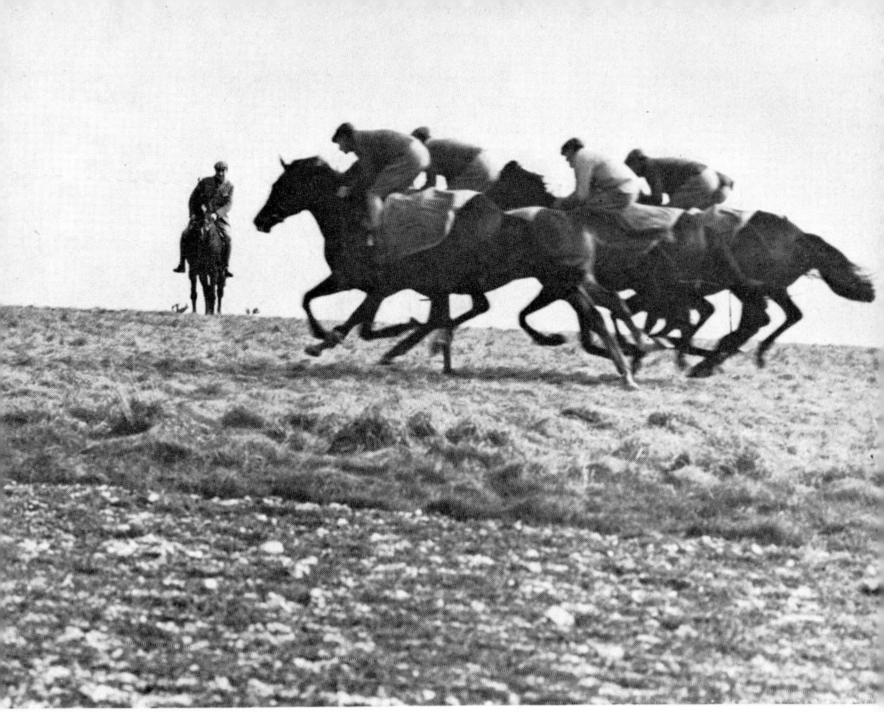

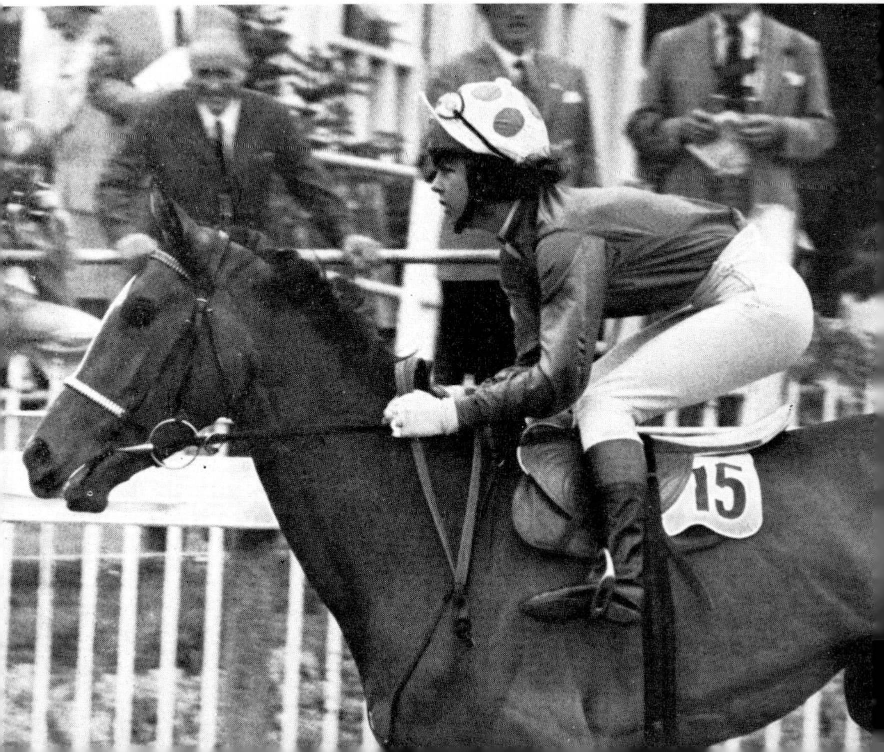
15

Top: National Hunt racing is a tough sport . . . (the 'Chair' at Aintree), but it has its more peaceful moments.
(*Below*) D. McCain and his horses on Southport sands.

in those it's just possible that you may graduate in time to becoming a 'jump jockey'. Even if you don't, however, you will find yourself being given the better horses to exercise and ride 'work' on, eventually, perhaps even horses to school. Steeplechasers, like their riders, have to learn their jobs, and if you become good at schooling horses over hurdles and fences, you will be an asset to any trainer.

Your wages will rise as you become more experienced, and according to your general ability and to what the Head Lad and the trainer consider to be your worth to the stable, and your possibilities for the future.

If it is the actual care and training of the horses which interests you most, you can rise from ordinary lad to Senior Lad, to Travelling Lad, or finally, perhaps, to Head Lad. Travelling Lad is an interesting position. You go with the horses to race-meetings all over the country and are entirely responsible for them while they are away. The job usually carries a house with it, if you are married or want to marry. If you are truly dedicated to the well-being and care of horses, and have a strong enough personality to cope with supervising the lads, you may in time become a Head Lad, the person who, under the trainer, is directly responsible for all the horses and the day-to-day running of the yard. He is also the person who may have to cope with owners if the trainer is away or busy. It is a well-paid and very responsible position, again with a house and 'perks' provided.

Becoming a Trainer

If you are interested in training itself: how horses are brought on from being inexperienced youngsters to mature animals capable of winning good races; how racing fitness is achieved and maintained and how individual horses are 'placed' (entered for the particular races in which they have the best chance of success); well, if you're intelligent and if financial circumstances permit, you may one day become a trainer yourself. Certainly, if you have kept your eyes, ears and mind open in a good National Hunt stable you will have a solid foundation on which to build.

Alternatively, if after a few years as a lad you don't want to continue along National Hunt lines you will find that you can always get a good position in private stables. You will have become a very competent groom, probably also a competent rider, and will have a sound knowledge of feeding and exercising. There are still a number of private people who keep hunters, maybe point-to-point some of them, who prefer to employ a really good male groom, if they can find one. Probably, in such a position, you would be on your own, or with a girl groom as your junior, and more than likely you would have a house provided. Incidentally if or when you decide to do this, do tell your trainer; don't just walk out on him. If you consult him and he thinks you're good at your job he may be able to help you to a good position.

How to Find a Stable

If you would like to get into a National Hunt stable the simplest way is to find out if there are such stables in your neighbourhood. Your School's Careers Officer should be able to tell you this. Write to the trainer, saying that you would like work as a lad, and ask if you can go to see him. If you live in a town or city your Careers Officer should still be able to give you suitable names. If he can't, write to the Jockey Club, 42 Portman Square, London W1, and ask if you could have the names and addresses of National Hunt trainers who might be willing to take you on.

Finally, if your sole ambition is to ride races over fences, and if you think you have the right qualities to make a jockey and could develop enough riding ability, there is a sort of back door into the profession which you may be able to open. Many National Hunt trainers and permit-holders are also farmers. If you can get taken on by one of them as a 'farm student', and if you are already a better than ordinary rider, you may be able to ride horses for him in point-to-points or hunter 'chases, as an amateur. This will give you experience and a start. Later, if you're good enough, which only time and plenty of rides will tell, you can, if you wish, turn professional. Fees for Steeplechase jockeys are (1975) £17·50 a ride plus a percentage of the stake money if you ride a winner.

Hunt Stables

If you work in National Hunt stables, even if you don't reach the highest pinnacles, there is always the chance that some of the glamour (if you think of it like that) of publicity will rub off on to you. Even if you never become a jockey and ride a winner you are more than likely to 'do' one, and find yourself leading it into the winner's enclosure, or following your trainer as he does so. Certainly, you will lead plenty of horses round the parade ring before very large crowds of people.

Hunt Service is far more private. If you succeed in becoming Huntsman, in 'carrying the horn', you will be a public figure only to your field – the followers of your Hunt. I would say this is definitely a career for those who want a country life, as well as a life with horses. Hunt Kennels (and stables) are not found in the middle of towns or cities. This doesn't mean you need to have been brought up in the country; only that you should have a genuine desire to live and work in it, through all its changing seasons, learning, as well as your job, something about nature and wild life and adapting yourself to the neighbourliness of country people. Moreover, think ahead to your adult life. Nowadays, relatively few children have the advantage of being brought up in the country with animals for company and all outdoors to play in; it might be pleasant if yours had this chance. It's up to you to decide. If you do want a country life, with a lot of riding thrown in, I think you would get a lot of satisfaction out of a career in Hunt Service.

Limited Openings

Openings, however, aren't endless, being limited by the number of Hunts in existence. However all Hunts do take on new staff from time to time, and all prefer to take on boys rather than girls, because no matter how good a groom or rider a girl may be, there is no future for her in professional Hunt Service. Most Hunts are willing to take on totally inexperienced boys, straight from school, if they're keen and willing to learn; and teach them to ride. Hunt horses are easier schoolmasters than National Hunt ones. For one thing, when they come up from grass in late summer, they want a lot of slow exercise, which is good practice for learner boys; for another, even when hunting fit, they are in regular work and consequently seldom 'silly' when being exercised.

If you went as a boy to a Hunt stable on leaving school, you would start at the minimum agricultural wage. If you didn't happen to live in the neighbourhood, you would be lodged, fed and generally cared for locally, part of your wage being taken for your keep. Your riding clothes would be provided free – breeches, jacket, riding mac, boots, leggings, hat, the lot.

The Way Up

When you start, you would be a sort of general dogsbody round the stables, where there may be from five to twenty or so horses kept. As you began to learn, you would progress to groom, or 'strapper', with your own two or three horses to 'do'. If your riding warrants it, you will next become second horseman, then second Whipper In, when, if you are married, you may also get a house and 'perks'. Next, first Whipper In, and, if you make the grade, Huntsman, hunting hounds, or Kennel Huntsman, hunting and in charge of the field in the Master's absence. The Huntsman is in overall charge of the stables and all employed therein.

There is no need to stay with the same pack all your life. A good first Whipper In may be invited to become Huntsman of another pack; good Huntsmen are much sought after, but don't always want to move. Some Hunt servants stay with the same Hunt all their lives. It will depend on how much you like the part of the country you're in, how you get on with your fellows, and the opportunities offered within the Hunt itself.

If you are interested, find out where your local Hunt Kennels are (the stables are there too); go along and try to see the Huntsman, see if he thinks they might take you on. If not, he may know of a neighbouring Hunt where you could start, or he may say they could take you at some definite date in the future.

I think that if you like the country and are mad keen on riding but not well enough off to have a horse of your own you would get a lot of pleasure, as well as a lot of riding, out of a career in Hunt Service, even though you had to work hard. Besides, if you want to, you can always move out of it into private stables. You will come in contact with a lot of well-to-do horsey people, who may own pointers and 'chasers as well as hunters, and who are always glad to get hold of a responsible, experienced groom, capable of looking after and riding high-class animals and turning them out in tip-top condition. One man I know has done just that. Starting as a 'dogsbody', he worked his way up through two different Hunts. Then, wanting more varied work, he went to a private stable, where he is now a highly competent and respected Head Groom and Stud Manager looking after hunters, point-to-point horses, 'chasers, brood mares, foals and young stock.

Both National Hunt and Hunt Service are careers which should give you a great deal of satisfaction. And both, for the sake of the welfare of all hunters and National Hunt horses, are well worth pursuing.

5   Flat-Racing Stables

Racing stables. Careers in these; culminating (with luck) in becoming a jockey, or rising through stable training to Head Lad, Travelling Lad, etc. Conditions, type of person wanted, etc.

There are probably quite a number of boys and young men who, watching racing on television or 'live', have dreamed themselves on to the backs of those elegant, not always predictable but always admirable animals whose lives are the business, and pleasure, of so many humans – racing Thoroughbreds. Those, that is, who haven't already dreamed themselves on to David Broome's or Harvey Smith's mounts!

Well, there's no harm in dreaming, you might become a second Lester Piggott. If you like horses, are keen on riding and not afraid of hard work, it is a dream that can can be given the chance of turning into reality if you become an apprentice in a racing stable. Beware of the Lester Piggott angle, though. Geniuses in any field are not two a penny, nor does anyone ever reach even the middle branches of the tree in any profession without a lot of hard work, as well as talent.

Apprenticeship

There is no short cut to becoming a jockey. It is no good presenting yourself to a trainer and telling him you want to ride his horses, even if you are a brilliant rider for your age and positively shrimp-like in stature. You must prove yourself through apprenticeship. You may be able to do this fairly quickly; on the other hand, you may never make the jockey grade at all. But even if you don't, and it is important to remember this, there are other jobs with futures in racing stables, if you work hard and have the racing bug in your veins. While the outsider probably always thinks of the jockey as the most important person in racing, this is true only on the day of the race. Without the skill of the trainer and his Head Lad, and the dedicated work of the lads and apprentices in the yard, the jockey would have no horse to ride.

Apprentices are usually taken on straight from school but they have to serve a short trial period before they are finally indentured: that is, before they sign on to stay with that particular stable for a period of three, five or seven years. The National Equestrian Centre, Kenilworth, Warwickshire, holds a limited number of courses for apprentices and would-be apprentices. The majority on these courses will have been nominated by trainers, but you, your School's Careers Officer, or your parents, can apply for a place before you go to a stable. This would not only provide you with useful experience, but also enable your instructors to assess whether they think you would make a jockey. You apply for these courses through the Jockey Club, 42 Portman Square, London W1; addressing your letter to Brigadier Kent, Apprentice Riding Courses. In the past, apprentices were always male. From 1975 onwards, girls are also eligible.

As an apprentice, you will be given free board and lodging, or the money to pay for them, sometimes in premises in or near the stables, sometimes in digs in the neighbouring town or village. You will also be given all your riding and racing clothes and a small weekly sum as pocket money.

In good stables, an apprentice 'does' two horses: that is, he looks after them entirely, rides them out to exercise and travels with them when they go racing. The more experienced lads help the apprentices with their riding and keep a sharp look-out for any with special talent, as does 'the boss' – the trainer himself. Holidays vary from stable to stable, but average a day and a half every other week-end, with a couple of weeks off at Christmas. The working day is usually from 7 in the morning until 12.30 with a long break in the afternoon; work again from 4 p.m. until 6 p.m., but the actual hours vary according to individual trainers' routines.

Opportunities to Ride

Unless an apprentice is particularly brilliant, he probably won't ride in a race for at least a year. It is not so easy to ride a fit racehorse in a race. For one thing, you as well as the horse must be fit, and if you have come from a town or city, as many apprentices do, this will take time, as it also takes time to acclimatize yourself to the different way of life.

If you are good, your trainer and his owners will be glad to let your ride, because apprentices claim 'weight allowances': the horses they ride carry less weight than those ridden by fully-fledged jockeys. These allowances are graded: seven pounds until you have ridden ten winners; five pounds up to fifty; three pounds to seventy-five; after which you can no longer claim an allowance, although you can still be an apprentice up to the age of twenty-three. There are some special races for apprentices; winning one of these doesn't count against your allowance total.

If you begin to make a name for yourself as an apprentice rider, you trainer will allow you to ride for other stables, but, as an apprentice, your riding fee will be paid to your trainer who will give you a proportion of it; what proportion will depend on how your apprenticeship has been drawn up. This is fair enough. After all, if you spend a lot of time riding for others, you won't have a lot left to work for your own trainer!

D

Riding fees for jockeys and apprentices are at the time of going to print £15 per ride. Jockeys also get $7\frac{1}{2}$ per cent of the winning stakes.

The Weight Problem

It isn't necessary to be very small to become a jockey: Piggott himself is quite tall. However it is a disadvantage to be the bulky, big-boned type, because you will find it harder to keep your weight down as you mature. Even if you do find yourself becoming too heavy, it need not be the end. If you are good, you can go over into jumping; the minimum weights carried by hurdlers and steeple-chasers being higher than the normal maximum flat-race weights.

And what if you don't make the grade as a jockey? If you want to stay in racing stables, as you probably will, you can become a lad, then you can work your way up, maybe to Travelling Lad, Head Travelling Lad, or even to that important person, Head Lad, who, as in National Hunt stables, is responsible, under the trainer, for the running of the stables, the welfare of the horses and the supervision of the staff.

Duties

As ordinary lad, you will probably begin on the minimum agricultural wage, possibly rather more, depending on your age. This will rise as you prove your worth. You will have your own horses to 'do', ride work on, and travel with and you will be expected to help the apprentices learn their job. You may also help with the breaking of young horses, which come to the trainer in the autumn of their yearling year, when they are about eighteen months old. The young horses are lunged before they are backed; the Head Lad, or the trainer himself, usually does this, or sometimes one of the most experienced lads. An apprentice generally does the first backing, because he's probably lighter than anyone else. Once backed, the young horses are walked and trotted quietly until they are settled enough to be taken out on the exercise gallops, always with an older horse leading them. This is work that goes on through the winter. It is interesting and important; the future of a young horse depends a great deal on how it has been handled, broken and backed.

As you work your way up, and if you are married, you will probably have a house provided. Head Travelling Lads are usually promoted from within the stable, Head Lads more often from other stables. Incidentally, there is nothing to stop you changing stables, but the Jockey Club, which is the ruling body of racing, demands that every lad changing his job has a reference from his previous employer. Racehorses are so valuable, this is an obvious necessity. A careless, irresponsible, or, worse, a bad-tempered lad can do a lot of harm to a horse.

Stable Lasses

Although until 1975 apprentices have always been male, for many years now a lot of 'lads' have in fact been 'lasses'. In all stables a good girl 'lad' is just as welcome as a boy; nor is there any reason why a girl should not get right to the top of the tree in this line. More than one stable has a girl, or rather a woman, Head Lad, and, as women are now officially entitled to hold trainers' licences, circumstances, money and ability permitting, there is nothing to stop a woman becoming a trainer. What the future holds for girl apprentices no one can yet say for certain.

In racing stables, girls do exactly the same work as boys. If you are a girl you should remember however, that for many years racing was a man's world and it's a tough one. You must accept this, and the fact that no one is going to make allowances, or make things easier for you, because of your sex.

Apprentices of both sexes, but especially you young men whose ambition it is to ride into the winner's enclosure; you should remember that only about 10 per cent of apprentices taken on actually make jockey grade, and of those only a few ever get into the big money. But then, that's the same in all professions: not everyone can get to the top. And though money is important, it isn't the most important thing in life. So long as you make enough to live on, surely what is important is to work at something you like doing, because then your work is also your pleasure.

How to Start

The best way to start in racing stables is to make contact with a particular trainer, either directly or through your School's Careers Officer. If there are racing stables in your district, find out the name of the trainer, write to him, giving plenty of details about yourself, and ask if you can see him. Enclose a stamped addressed envelope; this is polite, and will encourage a busy man to answer your letter promptly. If you know of no one to contact locally, and your School's Careers Officer can't help you, write to the Jockey Club, 42 Portman Square, London W1, explaining that you want to get into racing stables as an apprentice, or as a lad, if you have no race-riding ambitions. They will send you a list of trainers who may be able to take you on. It is then up to you to make the approach directly.

Racing Thoroughbreds are the most prized and valuable equines in the world and although there are Thoroughbreds in every country where racing flourishes, all stem from three stallions the Darley Arabian, the Godolphin Arabian and the Byerley Turk – imported into England between two and three hundred years ago, and bred to the best English mares of the time. The creation by our forbears of this superlative breed which, wherever its present domicile, can still correctly be called the 'English Thoroughbred', is one of the most remarkable achievements in the history of livestock breeding. Certainly it is one of which we as a people can be justifiably proud. There are, however, a great many people on the fringe of the racing world who have no contact with, knowledge of, or much real interest in, the animal that makes the sport possible. To them racing is either a pleasantly spectacular way of making (or losing) money, or a business in which if you can't make money legitimately you may perhaps do so by pulling a few fast ones here and there. If you decide to make your career in racing stables, you should beware of the latter; the jolly, affable types who cynically believe every man has his price and who may one day offer one to you, in return for some information or maybe a fiddle on some particular horse.

To work with racing Thoroughbreds calls for integrity, both to the animals themselves and to the men who created their breed; we owe them the duty of thinking always and above all of the preservation and furtherance of its excellence.

6 The Veterinary Profession and Animal Nursing

Veterinary surgery. Details of qualifications necessary before training; opportunities open (very wide range of these). Added to this, training as RANAs, Registered Animal Nursing Auxiliaries—mostly for girls.

You may not have thought of the profession of veterinary medicine and surgery as coming within the scope of a career with horses. In one sense, of course, it doesn't because the scope of the profession is far wider than the welfare of one particular animal or species; in another, it does, because just as in human medicine, once you have trained and qualified, you can go on to make one particular animal your special study. Even if you don't deliberately specialize, most veterinarian practices today have a large number of equine patients. If you take particular interest in them and become known as being 'good with horses', you will build an enviable reputation for yourself, and a successful practice.

Specialization

In human medicine, before you can specialize in whichever branch most interests you, you must first train for and obtain your general medical degree, so with animal medicine. Before you can begin to think of any kind of specialization, you must become a 'vet': that is, obtain your degree and become a Member of the Royal College of Veterinary Surgeons – MRCVS. To do so is not easy, any more than becoming a doctor is easy. To begin with, your academic qualifications need to be high: 'A' levels, or Scottish 'Highers', with emphasis on chemistry, biology, physics and mathematics. Competition to enter the profession is keen. For example, in one year at the Glasgow Veterinary College, there were 600 applicants for fifty places. There is, however, no sex discrimination; often up to half the students are women. A point here, though, is that women are not so suitable for practices dealing with large animals, simply because they are usually smaller than men and not so strong.

The Royal College

The controlling body of the veterinary profession is the Royal College of Veterinary Surgeons, 32 Belgrave Square, London SW1. The College recognizes the degrees granted by the six veterinary colleges in the United Kingdom which are each a part of the parent university. These are in England: London, Bristol, Liverpool, and Cambridge; and in Scotland: the Royal (Dick) Veterinary College, Edinburgh, and the Glasgow Veterinary College. The first degree which you will obtain at the end of your course of studies is Bachelor of Veterinary Medicine and Surgery, BVMS, which qualifies you to become a Member of the Royal College, MRCVS, and enables you to practice.

Naturally, you will get the usual student grants for the veterinary course, which lasts five years, during which you are, like all other students, an undergraduate of the university.

The major difference between the veterinary course and most others is that you have to spend a specified time doing practical work during the vacations. In your first and second years, when incidentally the course is much the same as that for medicine and dentistry, you will be expected to spend a total of eighteen weeks working on a farm, learning about animal care and feeding and having to look after animals yourself, under supervision. In your third, fourth and final years your vacations must be spent working as a student with a practising veterinary surgeon.

General Practice

When you are qualified you can, if you like, do what general practitioners used to do before the National Health Service: choose a nice part of the country with plenty of animals about, 'put up your plate' and hope for clients. However, this is risky! The most sensible thing to do is to go as an assistant to an established practice. If you got on well in one of the practices where you did your student 'practical', and your boss and his clients liked you, it would be a good start for you; perhaps if the practice was a large one you might work up to becoming a partner. But, in choosing your first job, you should remember that town and country practices are essentially different. Town ones are almost entirely confined to small animals: dogs, cats, budgerigars, hamsters, goldfish, etc. Country practices are more truly 'general', for although the majority of your patients will be the larger animals – cattle, pigs, sheep and horses – country people do keep small pets as well. If you are particularly interested in horses, as you probably are, do try to join a practice in a part of the country where there *are* horses! If you are lucky you might manage to find one in or near Newmarket, that Mecca of equine medicine.

General veterinary practice means a busy life, particularly in the country; whereas doctors can ask their patients to attend surgeries, you can only do this for small animal patients. Your district may be a large one, you will get to know its every lane and byway, finding your way to all the livestock-owning farms and houses. You will also get to know all the people in those farms and houses, and you will become an integral and important part of the community. As 'the vet', you will be asked to help with all sorts of local activities: give lectures to Young Farmers' Clubs, take part in Matters of Opinion, talk to pony and riding clubs, go as an attending vet to shows in the neighbourhood, where, as well as dealing with any accidents that may happen, you may be asked to measure ponies, check for lameness or disease, or help round-up recalcitrant cattle. In a town or city practice there obviously won't be so much visiting, most small animal patients will be brought to the surgery.

Post-graduate Work

However, about 40 per cent of the veterinarians who qualify don't go into general practice and, moreover, many do post-graduate training to obtain higher and more specialized qualifications. The post-graduate degrees which can be gained are: Doctor of Veterinary Medicine (DVM), Doctor of Veterinary Surgery (DVS), Master of Veterinary Medicine (MVM), or Ph.D. The Royal College also offers Diplomas in Veterinary Radiology and Veterinary Anaesthesia and the Diploma of Fellowship of the Royal Society (FRCVS). Also, if you are particularly interested in, and have a talent for, research work, certain colleges offer post-graduate courses in laboratory research, for which you will probably get an extra educational grant. There are many openings for really talented, qualified research workers.

If you like teaching and have the gift of being able to pass on knowledge, you could become a teacher or lecturer. There is always a demand for good teachers, both in this country and abroad, particularly in the developing countries, where British veterinarians have done, and are still doing, a great deal to help establish veterinary training colleges.

You can go into Government service and work in the Animal Health Division of the Ministry of Agriculture. This is important work, for the Division is responsible throughout the British Isles for the prevention and the control, should they occur, of notifiable diseases: foot-and-mouth, anthrax, brucellosis, and so on. It is also responsible for the inspection of markets, abbatoirs and the ports of entry of this country.

Then there is the Veterinary Investigation Service, which in England and Wales is controlled by the Ministry of Agriculture and in Scotland by the Agricultural Colleges. In this Service you act as adviser and consultant to the general practitioner, in much the same way as the specialist does in the medical profession.

And of course there are the many big Newmarket veterinary practices, which so definitely specialize in horses that they can hardly be called 'general'. If you can get into one of them, and perhaps have also done some special training in research, you may be able to get into the famous Newmarket Equine Research Station.

I would say that if you are compassionate towards all animals as doctors are compassionate towards us, the veterinary profession, even if you can't concentrate entirely on the horse, offers you a wide variety of interesting and worth-while career openings.

RANAs

There may be many of you who are deeply interested in veterinary work, but who feel that you could never achieve the rather high academic qualifications needed to become a practitioner. Don't despair, you can train to become a RANA, a Registered Animal Nursing Auxiliary. This is a fairly new subsidiary to the veterinary profession which is already proving itself to be of inestimable value.

It was in 1961 that the Royal College of Veterinary

Surgeons decided to start a scheme to train, and after training to keep a register of, animal nurses. To train to become a RANA you have to be seventeen years old and you need three 'O' levels. One of these must be English, and one of the others either mathematics or physical or biological science. It takes two years to train and to pass the two necessary qualifying examinations, but the training needn't be consecutive, and you are paid while you are doing it because your training consists of working as a student nurse with a practising veterinarian who is qualified to teach you. At least that is one way of training. Another is to train at a veterinary college, where you can attend the necessary lectures 'on the spot', and gain your practical nursing experience from the animals in for care or operation. There are also certain technical colleges where you can attend the lectures your training requires.

The curriculum is comprehensive. You have to study, and pass examinations in, anatomy and physiology, as well as know about the general care and feeding of different animals in sickness and in health. You also have to pass an examination in, and be able to administer, anaesthesia because one of a RANA's duties is to help during operations.

A Big Demand

There is a big demand for RANAs; large veterinary practices sometimes employ several. Their help is invaluable, not only during actual operations, but when animals are kept in for post-operative care or for long-term treatment. Up to the present, RANAs' work has been mostly with the smaller animals. There is no reason why it shouldn't spread to include the 'visiting' nursing care of larger ones, which are usually looked after on their owners' premises. As a paragraph in the Royal College's booklet about RANAs says: 'The scope of the work open to these people [RANAs] may be, or may become, quite wide. The standing of this relatively new cadre, in the eyes of the profession and the public, depends almost entirely upon the personal efforts of its members.'

Certainly, in the horse world of today, when so many owners are more or less inexperienced, trained help in nursing certain cases of sickness or injury would be most welcome. When there are enough RANA's, something like the District Nurse scheme for humans could be worked out, where a veterinary surgeon might be able to send a RANA to help clients with what may seem to them particularly difficult nursing problems: changing dressings, giving injections, or checking heart, pulse and respiration.

If you are interested in becoming a RANA, write to the Royal College of Veterinary Surgeons, and ask them to send you their booklet *Animal Nursing Auxiliaries*, together with a list of places in your vicinity where you could train. As there aren't enough RANAs to go round, once trained, you will be sure of a job. Moreover, like human nursing, it is a job you can always return to, wherever you may happen to be living.

7 Farriery and Saddlery

Farriery. Desperately important career; and nowadays well paid, and extremely interesting; also one in which one can be entirely 'one's own master' in the end. Saddlery. Another necessary and interesting profession vital to the horse world.

When considering careers with horses it would be wrong to think of farriery as a subsidiary profession. In fact, it is so important one can truly say that if there were no farriers there would be no riding, hunting, eventing, show-jumping, driving – the entire horse world would come to a standstill. Perhaps a few fortunate individuals who rode on nothing but grass might manage to keep going; but even they would find that their mounts did not go sound for very long if there was no one to trim, shape and generally care for their horses' feet.

The old saying 'No foot – no horse' is such a truism we tend to take it for granted; just as, if we are lucky enough to have a good farrier, we tend to take him for granted. This is thoughtless of us because the care and well-being of horses' feet are of vital importance not only to the horse, but to the rider, and this involves very much more than just being sure the animal has four shoes on.

Horses' shoes should fit them as comfortably as ours should fit us, possibly even more so when you consider the structure of a horse's foot and the work it has to do. Did you realize, for instance, that in the evolution of the horse, the digits which in us have stayed separate as fingers or toes have grown together to form the foot? The horny covering of the hoof being equivalent to our nails; the sole and the frog like the cushions of our fingers; the horse walking more or less 'on the points', as they call it in ballet. You probably do know that when a horse lands over a jump there is a fractional moment when the whole weight of his body (and of yours on top) is borne by one forefoot. Equally, that when galloping there is a moment when one forefoot carries all. Tie these facts to the structure of the foot, think of the weight and strain to which that foot is constantly being subjected, and you will understand how important it is that feet should be sound and healthy and that shoes should be as perfectly fitting, and as suitable to the work the horse has to do as possible.

Imagine yourself asked to run a mile in tight shoes, or to jump a ditch with shoes that stub your toes. You, of course, have a remedy – you can take your shoes off. The horse can't. It is therefore of vital importance to the horse world in general that so long as we use horses for our pleasure there should be enough trained farriers to ensure that our pleasure isn't the horse's distress.

A Necessary Career

Considering all these things, I can think of few more necessary careers than the profession of farriery; which I hasten to say doesn't mean you have to be a great muscular individual with brawny arms, nor that you have to spend your days sweating profusely as you swing your hammer or blow up your forge. It doesn't take enormous strength to be a blacksmith. It is knack and know-how that do the trick, as we have probably all discovered in our time, struggling to take off a loose shoe, and spending what seems like hours over what takes the farrier a few seconds. Nor do you have to get particularly dirty fitting shoes or 'turning' (making) them at your forge.

Required Knowledge

What it does take, as does every profession connected with horses, is dedication combined with a real interest in, and feeling for, the horse as an animal, and the right sort of temperament – calm, but firm and patient. A nervous, impatient, or hot-tempered person will never make a really successful farrier. It also takes a fair amount of intelligence, because you have to know a great deal more than how to make, put on, or take off, a set of shoes. To begin with there are many kinds, types and weights of shoe. Before you become qualified to make and fit them, you must know something of the anatomy of the horse in general, and in particular the workings of the tendons, ligaments and joints of the legs, and the structure of the foot. You must also know the diseases of the foot: how to diagnose them and which can be helped, or cured, by the shaping of the foot, or by corrective shoeing. You must know how a horse should stand correctly, in natural balance, and how the feet must be trimmed to enable him to do so, 'bearing evenly' on all four. You must also know how faulty action can be helped by the shaping of the foot, something which is particularly important when dealing with young horses. So many of them are allowed to mature with badly shaped feet and consequently faulty action because their feet have never had skilled attention. In fact, qualified farriers are truly 'veterinarians of the foot'. They are living up to both definitions of the word 'farrier', which, if you look it up in the *Oxford Dictionary*, means 'horse-doctor' as well as 'shoeing-smith'. So, you see, there's rather more to the profession of farriery than you may have thought, watching a blacksmith at his job, trimming, shaping, fitting and shoeing with apparent ease.

Training Schemes

If you want to train as a farrier, the first thing you have to do is find a Master Farrier who is willing to take you on as an apprentice. Entry into the profession is through a four years' apprenticeship. If you have no connections in the horsey world, and don't know any farriers, your School's Careers Officer may be able to help you; or you can go and see your local Small Industries Organizer (you can get his address from the Youth Employment Bureau). While you are looking for a Master, you, your headmaster or your parents should also approach the Local Education Authorities to see if they will give you a Further Education grant while you are apprenticed. When you have found a Master write to the Worshipful Company of Farriers, addressing your letter to R. N. Clarke, Esq., Field Officer, 58 Hall Park Drive, West Park, Lytham, Lancs., asking to be sent the Company's apprenticeship application form. Apprenticed under the Company's scheme, you will receive a standard weekly wage which will rise as your training proceeds. The Company also gives grants to help you with books, tools and clothing. During your apprenticeship you must attend at least one course of farriery each year. These are held at different schools approved by the Company, one being the Royal Army Veterinary Corps Training Centre at Melton Mowbray.

At the end of your fourth year you should have reached a certain standard and be able to pass the examination required to become a Registered Shoeing Smith (RSS); this qualifies you, if you so wish, to set up on your own. There are two further certificates which you can obtain as time goes on: Associate of the Farriery Company of London (AFCL) and Fellow of the Worshipful Company of Farriers (FWCF). At any time after you have become an RSS you may in your turn, and with the approval of the Worshipful Company, take on and train apprentices.

A Good Living

With the enormous increase in the horse population there is today a very good living to be made as a farrier. Two farriers I know well, one elderly, one much younger. Both say that there is not only enough work for them, but a great deal more than they can possibly take on, even if, working for themselves, they do many more weekly hours than the statutory forty.

A major difference between farriery today and in the past is that now most people expect their farriers to come to them. It is therefore almost imperative that as well as your home forge, where you make your shoes, you have a small portable one which you take with you in your van to do hot shoeing for your clients. But it isn't necessary to go into business on your own; there are, as well as partnership possibilities, quite a number of salaried positions for farriers. Most racing stables like to have their own resident farrier, so do many big studs and showing stables.

For the sake of all horses, I do hope that some of you, wondering what you are going to do in life, will consider becoming qualified and efficient farriers. If you like an outdoor life and are interested enough in horses to be willing to learn how to understand them as well as how to shoe them, I am sure that this very necessary profession offers you a rewarding career.

Saddlery

To me, saddlery is a most fascinating craft. I love the look and the feel of good-quality, well-kept leather. I enjoy cleaning tack, and not only because I know that if I don't, it will not last, or be so comfortable, or so safe, for me or the horse. I enjoy it because I like to pick up clean, supple reins. I like my horse's head to look through a neat, clean bridle, and it gives me really intense pleasure to see the

E

mahogany glow that years of use and cleaning will bring up on the leather of a good saddle.

Maybe you are a leather fan too. If you are, I'm sure you must, as I do, admire the workmanship of the good saddler, the inheritor from a long line of master craftsmen of a skill that though the centuries has contributed so much to our pleasure and comfort on horseback. Not to mention his many contributions to the well-being and comfort of the horse: tendon boots, brushing boots, hock boots, night rugs, day rugs, New Zealand rugs, padded rollers, breaking tackle – the list is endless. Even if you are one of those people who take your tack for granted, and think it rather a nuisance having to clean it, you must admit that without it you would be hard put to make good use of your horse. Certainly, the craft of saddlery has been a recognized and organized craft for far longer than most of us, with our up-to-date spring-tree saddles, probably realize.

The Saddlers' Company

The Worshipful Company of Saddlers is the oldest of the present-day Livery Companies of the City of London. The earliest document in the Company's possession goes back to 1160 and is a Convention between the Convent of the Church of St Martin-le-Grand and the Guild of Saddlers, in which there is already mention of 'customs of old', from which it would appear that the Company was originally an Anglo-Saxon craft Guild. The first Charter was granted to the Company by Edward I in 1272, then came the Incorporation Charter granted by Richard II in 1395, the provisions of which were amended or ratified by subsequent monarchs until James I, whose Charter of 1607 is in force today.

If you like working with your hands it might interest you to train to become a Master Saddler; there is a good living to be made, and good business opportunities, in saddlery today. If you did, it would surely give you a remarkable sense of historical continuity to belong to a group of people whose craft association goes back through eight centuries.

Apprenticeship

There are different ways of learning, or becoming apprenticed to, the craft. First, if you are still at school, you should consult your School's Careers Officer and your headmaster, because it is likely that if you decide to train seriously you will be given a Further Education grant to do so. Also as one of the ways to learn is to work with a Master Saddler, the Careers Officer may know of one who would be willing to take you on. He will do so either as a 'learner-worker', when he will pay you a wage, small at first but rising as you become more skilled and of more use to him; or as an apprentice, when you will sign an agreement to remain with him for a stated number of years, probably five, and probably pay him an apprenticeship fee. Training in the workshops of a Master Saddler you would literally learn as you worked, starting with the simplest of stitching repair jobs until at the end of your time you were competent to make, as well as to repair, all the assorted articles of tack, even some of the clothing, needed by the contemporary horse, saddles probably excepted. Today very few saddles are made by hand, by one individual, from start to finish. While the best may be put together by hand, more generally the various parts will be cut out by one man, or group of men, and assembled and finished by others. Nevertheless, you will know all about the anatomy of a saddle, having had dozens to re-line and re-stuff, and probably quite a few to take apart for a tree repair, and put together again.

One advantage of training in an actual saddler's business and shop is that as well as learning your craft you will get an idea of how such a business is run to make a profit, which will help you if one day you want to set up on your own. You will learn which wholesale firms are the best to deal with, and what lines, apart from actual saddlery and stable equipment, it might pay you to stock in your shop. Leather handbags perhaps, or dog accessories, or luggage, or maybe, in certain parts of the country, sporting goods. And as a good saddler's clients frequently wander into the workshop, either with their repairs or just to have a chat and a look round, you will get used to meeting people and talking to them, recognizing them next time they come and remembering their names if you can. Remembering who people are is good public relations in any business. Working saddlers often take stands or set up tents or caravans to display their stock at shows, events and major riding and Pony Club activities. Again good public relations, and good experience for you if you are taken along. Many saddlers, if one of their best clients wants a new saddle, will take several to the client's home, to try on the horse. If you go too you will learn a lot about the proper fitting of a saddle to both horse and rider. Then there is the second-hand trade, which is part of every working saddler's business. Obviously, if Mrs Jones's little girl outgrows her pony, she will outgrow her saddle as well, so Mum will want to turn it in against the cost of a new one. It will probably want a bit of work done on it before re-selling, but there are always customers for good second-hand saddles. So, you will learn how to reckon up the cost of work in time and material, deduct it from what you will get for the saddle, and know what you can offer Mrs Jones, at the same time leaving a little in hand for the business.

Most interestingly, your Master may at times be asked to make special tack for a special purpose, or for an animal that is too big or too small to be fitted from stock.

Maybe a lungeing cavesson for a Shetland pony, or show-ing gear for a Clydesdale stallion, or, with the present revival of interest in driving and the shortage of harness, a set of driving harness. My saddler, for instance, was asked not long ago by the staff at Balmoral to make a very special set of driving harness for them to present to Prince Philip on the occasion of the Royal Silver Wedding, an enviable commission, to which no doubt everyone in the workroom contributed something.

However, as it isn't always easy to find a Master saddler able to take you on exactly at the moment you want to start your training, let us look at other ways of learning the craft.

Career Assistance

The Cordwainers Technical College, 182 Mare Street, Hackney, London E8, as well as courses in all kinds of leatherwork, runs a Rural Saddlers' Course. If you pass the theoretical and practical examinations at the end of this course the Worshipful Company of Saddlers can help you to continue your training by giving you a bursary. If you write to the Registrar of the College he will send you full details of the course. You can also learn saddlery and leatherwork at the City and Guilds of London Institute, and at the Walsall School of Arts and Crafts; again, if you pass the necessary examinations at either, the Worshipful Company can help you to further training. The Company can also sometimes pay apprenticeship fees for young men whose parents cannot afford to pay them. However you decide to train, it would be to your advantage to write to the Secretary of the Worshipful Company of Saddlers, 9 St Thomas Street, London SE1, and ask for whatever in-formation and help he can give you.

Walsall, incidentally, is the heart of the wholesale saddlery business in Britain; you can, of course, take a job in the workshops of one of the big manufacturing firms there. But if your aim is to become a fully competent working saddler, if you cannot train under or become apprenticed to an individual Master, you would be better advised to start by taking a technical training course.

8 Working on Your Own

Running one's own business . . . deciding the best 'line' for one's self, and the district in which one lives. Problems. Staffing. Training of students. Public relations – with local councils, Rights of Way, neighbours, etc. Riding clubs, Pony clubs and help to them. Sidelines, such as buying for clients – liveries etc.

Running a Riding School

If you have good qualifications, are ambitious, and finances permit, it is more than likely that one day you may want to run your own riding school, with your own horses, clients, pupils and students. A natural and worthy ambition, specially if you are a good teacher, so don't think I'm just being elderly and depressing if I advise you not to hurry into taking this important step. First, because the more experience you can get beforehand, the better. Second, because far more is involved than simply being able to afford to buy a certain number of horses and ponies and their tack; and, third, you need to find someone who is prepared to go in with you – perhaps a friend who could be a partner, or who is keen enough to be willing to help you for, at first, not very much money. No one, however dedicated and hard-working, can possibly run even a small riding school entirely on their own. If you try to do so you will find you never have even half a day off, far less a holiday; and what happens if you become ill? Horses can't be left to look after themselves. And if you start by taking a working pupil or student, though they will give you a lot of help, it won't be quite fair to them as you will not have the time to teach them properly. You may, of course, be able to afford to employ a qualified assistant. If so, do be sure that it is someone who is really congenial, and is prepared to stay with you for at least a year. It makes a great difference to a new school to have someone working with you whom clients can think of as a friendly 'permanent'.

My advice to anyone starting would always be – start small. It is far better to have more clients than you can cope with than it is to have to feed half a dozen horses doing nothing. It is also easier to increase your size and scope as time goes on, than it is to cut down. Besides, there are a number of things other than horses and tack on which you will need to spend money before you start and so you won't be able to afford a lot of horses at first, unless you have wealthy parents, or have been lucky enough to find yourself a rich 'backer'.

Schools and the Law

Nowadays every riding school or establishment of any kind to which people pay money for riding has by law to be licensed by the local County, Town, Borough or District Council. Unfortunately, this law is sometimes evaded, and 'wild-cat' places calling themselves 'riding schools' still do exist. But as you will want to run a reputable school, approved by one of the official 'horsey' bodies, the BHS, the ABRS or the Ponies of Britain, you must first apply for, and obtain your official Licence. Your premises and your animals will be inspected by a veterinary surgeon appointed by the Licensing Authority of your district. Your premises needn't be grand but they will have to conform to certain standards. Your boxes must be large enough for the animals to move about in freely, and lie down in comfortably. Ten foot square is sufficient for ponies; ten foot by twelve foot or twelve foot square for horses. If you use some stalls, as well as boxes, these should be wide enough, and divided by partitions high enough to stop

Hunt Service is essentially for those who want a country life as well as a life with horses. (*Below*) To produce a show hunter calls not only for riding skill but for a high standard of horse-mastership. Roy Trigg on Aristocrat.

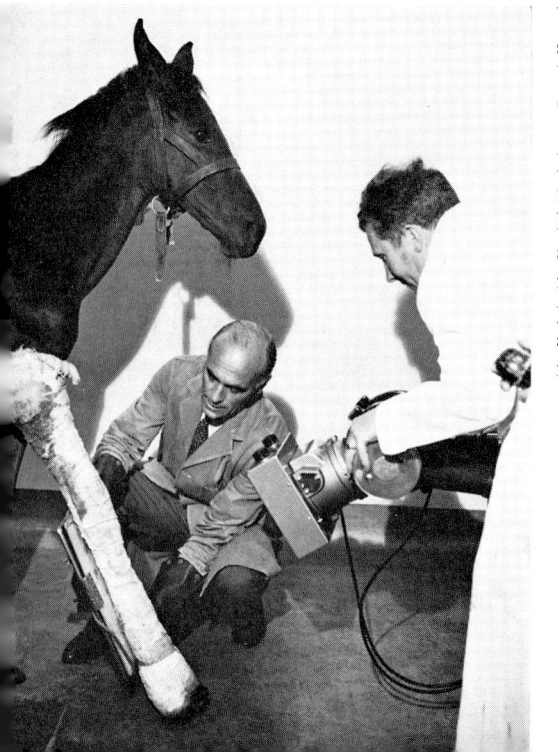

You need to be fit, to show 'in hand'. A Welshman shows a Welsh Cob.

(*Left*) Veterinary surgeons X-ray a young horse recovering from a broken leg. Time was when such an injury would have meant death; now, this youngster will one day be able to move again as freely as the cob above.

A Master Farrier at his forge, and (*below*) an apprentice farrier shoeing

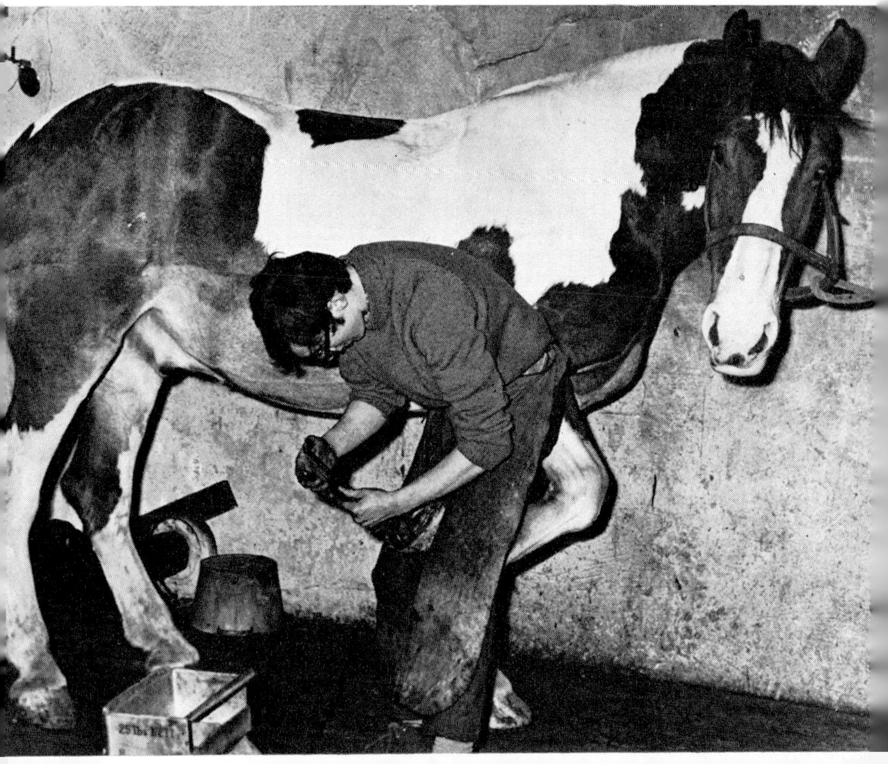

In riding, there is no age limit: (*above*) Mrs Lorna Johnstone
on El Farucco. Mrs Johnstone celebrated her seventieth
birthday during the 1972 Olympics, where she was the most
successful member of the British Dressage Team. (*Below*) Nor
is there ever an end to the pleasure of watching mares and
young foals.

the animals getting at each other over the top. You should have one box some way from the others which you can use for sickness or isolation, or a barn or shed suitable for this purpose. You need a water supply to the stables; a stand-pipe in the yard will do. If your stabling is very close to the back door of your house, you may get by with using water from a scullery or back kitchen. You need fire extinguishers, a room or shed for your tack and for your hard feeds, which must be stored in mouse- and rat-proof bins. You also need a barn, shed or loft for storing hay and straw; incidentally, the larger this storage space is, the better, for whatever hay may cost, it is always cheaper to buy it in bulk early in the year. Never worry about having too much; good hay will keep from one year to the next.

Insurance and Accommodation

You also need, by law, an insurance policy to cover Third Party risks. Be sure you carry enough cover. You may never have a claim made against you, but if you do, it is foolish to have too little cover. Whether or not you insure your horses is up to you. Personally, unless you have a particularly valuable animal, or live in a part of the country where grass sickness if prevalent, I think, for riding school horses, it is hardly worth while. As you will probably have had no previous experience of insurance, I would write to the British Horse Society and ask for their advice, and for the names of agents.

You have probably often seen, in stables, notices to the effect that riders do so at their own risk. This, in fact, means precisely nothing. If a rider has a serious accident which he can prove is due to negligence on your part you can be sued for damages. The important thing, therefore, is to see that you never give cause for anyone to claim negligence against you. Riders must wear hats. Your tack must be well kept, particularly girths, stirrup leathers and all buckles and fastenings. And if you ever had the misfortune to have an accident your insurance company would be rather annoyed if they discovered you had sent a ride out in charge of someone under sixteen years of age. Or, for that matter, that you had let a novice rider out on a horse you knew was traffic shy or reared or bolted.

Those are the basics. If you want to insure your premises, it's up to you, – I think you should.

Now, accommodation: You may be able to afford to have boxes specially put up; many firms make excellent prefabricated ones, most will erect them for you, and there is a slight discount the more you order. The most expensive part of this is often the laying of the concrete bases. Of course, if you take over a going concern, all you will need to do is check the condition of everything, or you may where you can convert existing sheds and outhouses, if not into all the stabling you need, at any rate into storage sheds. You should also have some grazing facilities, if not of your own, a field or fields you can rent from a neighbouring farmer. Ponies are better out than in when they are not working. It is also good for stabled horses to be turned out now and then, weather permitting, for a graze and a roll. Fields must have water; either a stream or a container of some sort which you must keep filled with fresh, clean water. Fencing must be safe, and gates have proper 'horse-proof' fastenings; it is surprising how quickly some horses learn how to lift an ordinary latch or to slip a bolt! Unless you can afford a covered school, which naturally everyone hopes to achieve one day, you must have a suitably flat, well-drained space which you can use as an arena for lessons. Actually, even if, or when, you have an indoor school, an outdoor arena ai advisable. Horses, especially young ones, can become too accustomed to working within the safety of four walls, so can people. A horse can behave like an angel in the school and like a maniac outdoors, if he is not used to it. In the same way, pupils who appear to be calm, cool and in total control inside, can lose their heads, their positions and finally their seats when there are no walls to confine them!

Buying Horses

There are, you see, quite a lot of things to think about before you buy your animals. Here, I would advise you to be very choosy and very practical. You don't want a stable full of madly classy animals that are too much for your average client or pupil; nor do you want a collection of slugs. You want reliable, well-mannered, traffic-proof horses and ponies, with sensible temperaments that allow them to suffer fools, if not gladly, at least without rebellion as well as to be schooled to quite high standards of performance. First crosses, either Thoroughbred or Arab, of any of the larger Mountain and Moorland breeds make good types if you can find them; active, willing, with pony sense allied to TB or Arab scope and action, they are usually good doers and easy to keep in condition. Until you have been established some time, and have a good idea of the general standard and potential of your clients and pupils, I wouldn't go for Thoroughbreds; half or at the most three-quarter bred will give plenty of scope. What you really must have, though, is one real weight carrier: a sensible cob of about 15.2 is probably the answer. Never mind his breeding, or up to a point his looks, so long as he can cope with the client who, after booking his ride or his lesson, says: 'Oh, I suppose I ought to tell you, I weigh sixteen stone. . . .' There are more of these than you think! So long as your cob is a perfect gentleman (or lady) and not too enormous in height, you don't have to keep him only for your heavyweights; a cob is a gay, cheerful ride for anyone, and usually a careful and reliable jumper.

Children's Ponies

Children's ponies are a problem. You have to have them, or at any rate one of them, but in term time, particularly winter term time, you may not have many child riders. To start with, the best thing may be to have one real 'tiny', of 12 hands or so, and another of around 13 hands, which can also carry a small, light adult. The 'tiny' mustn't be too wide, nor too sluggish, nor too gay; the last thing it must ever want to do is 'dump' its rider! And though it's nice if 'tiny' can be good-looking, what really matters is its temperament; it must not only accept children, but appear actually to *like* them. Because what small children enjoy almost as much as riding is being able to handle ponies, to go into their boxes and feed and groom them, tack them up, and un-tack them. All of which is extremely good for the children, so long as you take the trouble to show them how to do these things the right way. Incidentally, 'tiny' must also lead well and briskly from a larger horse, neither pushing himself forward nor dragging back so that you have to play him at the end of the lead-rein like a salmon on a line. If you can teach 'tiny' to lunge reliably, with a child on top, then you will really have a paragon of all the virtues.

Exactly how many and what kind of animals you keep will naturally depend a lot on where you set up your school, and how many and what kind of clients and pupils you expect to have. Also, of course, it will depend on your own preferences for certain breeds and types. To get your Licence, however, and to obtain BHS, ABRS or PoB approval, *no horse or pony which you use for lessons or for taking clients out hacking may be under four years old.* Basically, this is a humanitarian law, designed to protect horses and ponies from being worked too young. It is also very sensible, because it just is not possible to teach someone to ride on a young, unschooled horse. It does not, however, prevent you from taking young horses to 'make and school', provided you keep this part of your business separate, and do not use the young horses as mounts for your clients.

Remunerative Sidelines

Which brings me to an important point, which is, that it is very difficult to make a riding school pay unless you have one or two extra activities, or sidelines.

One sideline is to take liveries. Nearly everywhere there are horse-owners who for one reason or another are finding it difficult to look after their animals themselves, and who are glad to put them at good livery. Provided you charge realistically, liveries provide a useful regular income. Naturally, what comes in goes out again almost at once, but, at any rate, it is coming in. There are three kinds of livery: full, half and a sort of in between one we can call 'three-quarter'. Full livery is when you look after the horse entirely, exercising it when the owner cannot, the exercising being done by yourself or a qualified assistant. Half livery is when you look after the horse entirely, but are allowed to use it in your school when the owner doesn't want to ride. The in-between, or three-quarter, one is when you feed and stable the horse, but the owner 'does' it; grooms it, mucks it out, and beds it down. Owners are always responsible for shoeing and any veterinary bills. With the prices of everything rising all the time, it is impossible to give you a rate which will be valid at the time you read this; it may help you to work it out if I say that in 1975 full livery would be at least £15 a week; the others, in proportion.

Charges

While talking of money; don't think, if you are starting a new school, that in order to get custom you must offer cut rates. If you do, it will only make knowledgeable people think that you can't be doing your horses properly; and if the unknowledgeable don't want to pay what you ask, you are better off without them. Exactly what you charge will depend on where you are situated and what you have to offer; but if you want to make a living, and keep your horses fed, you must relate your charges sensibly to your overheads – the current cost of feeding stuffs, what you may be paying in wages, and, of course, your own time.

Making Young Horses

Another sideline is taking young horses, to 'make and school'. As there are far too few people with the knowledge and competence to do this it can be financially rewarding as well as intensely interesting, particularly if you are really good and make a reputation for yourself producing well-schooled animals. If you are specially interested in this sideline, then you want to be sure that whoever is working with you is equally dedicated to teaching human pupils; young horses take up a lot of time. It is probably wise, until you have a large and flourishing establishment, never to take on more than two young ones at a time. The most irritating part of this business is that some owners have the idea that a hitherto unbroken horse, possibly even an almost unhandled one, can be turned out a reliable, mannered ride in a few weeks. On the whole, people are becoming a little more educated about 'breaking', but beware of committing yourself to doing too much in too short a time. If an owner will only let you have an unbroken horse or pony for, say, three weeks, they must be made to understand it may possibly be 'backed' at the end of that time, but by no means 'schooled'. On the other hand, with a horse that is already backed and going freely, you can do quite a lot in three weeks' concentrated schooling. The dream is an owner who sends in a well-handled youngster to break, make and school with no time limit attached. The nightmare is being sent a terrified, mixed-up youngster whose inexperienced owner, by attempting unsuccessfully to break it, has turned it into a neurotic problem. This, I may say, will probably happen to you quite often, and though the incompetence that produced the neurosis may make you angry – and sad – if you can sort the unfortunate animal out, it will give you great satisfaction.

Buying and Selling

Most riding schools do a certain amount of buying and selling. I hesitate to call it dealing, because it usually consists of finding a particular   horse or pony to suit a particular client, something which the client's riding teacher is obviously well qualified to do. To make a success of this sideline, you must be scrupulously honest in your interpretation of the word 'suit'. A gay, highly bred five-year-old pony is not going to suit a slightly nervous, not very competent child rider, even if its parents want to buy it because it's expensive, and they think their little darling may win prizes on it. A horse that may be a charming ride but is almost impossible to catch isn't going to make the perfect companion to an elderly lady rider who has to keep it out. A fairly competent teenager who wants to start some modest show-jumping will be far better with a middle-aged, even elderly, animal that knows its job and can teach her, than with a youngster, however brilliant its potential. She won't know enough to bring it on, and in the process of trying will probably frighten herself off horses for life. If you make a success of suiting horses to people, and I may say it takes strength of mind sometimes to resist the temptation to make a good sale to the wrong person, your name will be passed on by your clients to friends, and friends of friends, *ad infinitum,* till you find yourself with the enviable reputation of being someone who can always 'find the right one'.

Working Pupils

To call taking students or working pupils a sideline is not really accurate, because to do so is more or less an economic necessity nowadays. If you have gone into business with a friend as partner or helper, or you have been able to afford to start with a qualified employee, then you can take on a working pupil or student immediately. It is extremely important however that you take the time and the trouble to really *teach* them. Far too many working pupils are treated as general dogsbodies; while they are expected to work in return for their instruction, they must get that instruction, in riding and in stable management. The latter can be far more wearing and trying to the temper than teaching them to ride. For one reason, it is always so much quicker to do something oneself than to explain it to someone else; for another, the majority who start in stables are fearfully untidy, have no idea of method, and little thought for the cost of things. When you are training you will probably think your instructors are awful bores, the way they go on about being tidy and putting everything back in the right place. Go into business yourself and when you have to pay for all your stable equipment you will be driven crazy by the amount of money carelessness can cost you. Curry-combs found in mangers; hay-nets tied up wrongly and pulled into holes; head-collars left lying on the stable floor to be trodden on; hoof-picks lost and turning up in the manure heap; saddle soap on the tack-room floor; brooms left out in the rain to become sodden; taps left running and lights left on in the boxes. ('Do the horses want to *read*?' I've heard myself saying.) There is also the time wasted by inattention to detail: children's ponies tacked up with leathers long enough for a six-footer and five-inch irons; a fat horse with a girth in the bottom holes and a thin one with the girth too slack in the top ones; the German snaffle you want for a young horse out on a cob taking an elderly gentleman a pleasant hack; the lunge rein put away with knots in it and the lunge whip fallen down behind the corn bin . . . one could go on for ever! Teaching tidiness, method and attention to detail is far more exhausting than giving half a dozen riding lessons or wrestling with a young horse on the lunge, but it has got to be done, for your students' sakes and for your own, or whatever profits you do make will go on repairs and replacements, or on paying for a psychoanalyst for yourself!

Public Relations

Well those are some of the things you have to think about on the working side of setting up a riding establishment of your own. But there are other angles – public relations, for one. If there seems to be nice riding country roundabout, you must find out who it belongs to, and if they will allow you to ride over it, or part of it. If they do, but with certain conditions or restrictions, be sure you stick to them. Find out from the local County Council about the official 'Rights of Way'; in England, most Councils keep a map of these. In Scotland it is rather more difficult to ascertain what are established Rights of Way and what are simply tracks or paths used habitually by the local people. If in doubt, always contact the landlord, who may be a private person, or a public body, like the Forestry Commission. Good manners and tact will go a long way towards making you a welcome newcomer to a district.

There is probably a local branch of the Pony Club. Find out who the District Commissioner is, and send him or her a notice about your school, asking if you can be of help. As you are qualified to instruct, you will be welcomed

F

with open arms. The same goes for riding clubs, except that if there isn't one already in existence you will probably find yourself landed with starting one! These activities will bring you social contacts, just as hunting will, if there is a Hunt in your district and you can afford to go out now and then. Social contacts can be very useful. But never forget that you are a professional, and as such cannot afford to give your services, or the use of your amenities, jumps, arenas, covered school if you have one, for nothing.

Starting Your Own Stud

Oddly enough, starting a stud, or more accurately starting to breed horses or ponies, is so much simpler than setting oneself up in any kind of riding establishment, that people tend to do it almost by mistake. They 'put the old mare in foal' without stopping to think seriously of the complications and responsibilities involved. Therefore before we discuss some of the basics of commercial breeding do let me warn you against starting 'by mistake'. Don't put the old mare in foal unless you really want the foal and are prepared to cope with rearing, weaning and feeding it, and seeing that when you sell it, if you do, it goes to a proper home. I can think of nothing more pitiful than the fate of the hundreds of foals born every year whose owners only realize after the dear old mares have produced them that they are a liability they can neither afford, nor are equipped to deal with

Facilities

However, if you really want to go in for breeding and to have a small stud of your own, we will take it for granted that you have thought seriously about it, and that you have the necessary amenities, the most important being land. With a riding school, or any other kind of horsey establishment, if the worst comes to the worst and you lose all your grazing you can stable your horses until you find something else. If you want to breed you must have land, either your own or land of which you have definite security of tenure. It doesn't need to be very rich land, you can always improve your pasture year by year, and, anyway, a good acreage of rough is an advantage. But all must be well and safely fenced; this is vital for foals and young stock. You will also need boxes, two will do to start with, for foaling if necessary, and for your weanlings to go into at night during the first winter of their lives, and, of course, storage space for your fodder and straw. However, as you probably won't even contemplate breeding unless you live on a farm or a smallholding, or have the use of part of either, or live in a house with maybe a couple of paddocks and some outbuildings, none of these should be a problem.

The most important thing to decide is what breed you are going to go in for. You probably have your favourite; we all have. But as few of us nowadays can afford to embark on any project purely for fun, you must stop to consider whether that favourite breed is likely to be commercially successful. You won't be able to keep all your young stock, will you be able to sell them reasonably well? No one can foretell the future these days, but you must use a bit of foresight and not just jump on the bandwagon of whatever breed seems to be making high prices at the time. For example, a few years ago Shetland ponies were fetching very high prices indeed, with the result that far too many people started breeding far too many ponies, not all of the best quality, and prices dropped.

Marketable Stock

Active riding horses of between fifteen and sixteen hands, with good bone, substance and temperament, will always find a market. So will registered animals of any of the nine native Mountain and Moorland breeds, for all are hardy, good doers, and relatively inexpensive to keep. These are points much in their favour when it comes to selling as the cost of keep seems to rise each year. They are also versatile; the larger breeds, Connemara, Fell, Dale, Highland, Welsh Cob and, up to a point, New Forest, all make good rides for both children and adults, the Connemara perhaps outstanding in this respect; while there's a steady demand for Highlands, Fells and Dales from holiday riding and trekking centres. All can also be broken to harness; here Welsh Cobs are outstanding, having proved themselves of the highest class in International Driving Competitions. From the breeder's angle, these large Mountain and Moorlands have a further advantage; their mares, if you cross-breed them with Thoroughbreds or Arabs, will produce first-class riding horses. Incidentally, those first-crosses put back to a TB may well give you an animal in the four-figure class.

Riding Ponies

If you want to breed children's ponies you probably think at once of Welsh Mountains. Personally, however, I feel that there are already so many successful and long-established studs breeding these lovely little aristocrats of the small pony world that you would find it both difficult and expensive to compete with them. The same applies to the larger Welsh, the Section Bs, and certainly to riding ponies, the breeding of which takes a great deal of experience, skill, capital with which to start, and luck to make the top grade. I would be more inclined to choose Exmoors or Dartmoors. Both make good children's ponies, and will cost you less to buy initially, and if, later on, you want to try your hand at producing riding ponies, you can put your mares to riding pony, small Thoroughbred, or Arab stallions.

Having decided on your breed, write to the Secretary of that particular Breed Society (which it will be both useful and tactful to join), and ask if you can have a list of studs and owners who may have stock for sale. Then contact them, and ask if you can visit. Meantime, try to see as many examples of your chosen breed as you can. Go to shows and watch their classes being judged and get an eye for them, so that when people show you animals they have for sale you will have a picture in your mind of what you want.

Foundation Mares

I would say that to start a stud you want two females. One can be quite an elderly mare; age doesn't matter with mares, they will go on breeding well into their twenties, and if she is a proven breeder you are less likely to be confronted with foaling problems in your first season. She could be a mare already in foal, but then you would miss the pleasure of selecting her mate yourself. The other female could be a three-year-old filly, or a two-and-a-half-year-old if you buy in autumn. As, however, she will be a maiden when you send her to the stallion you do run the slight risk of her not holding to service, or of her having difficulty with her first foal. I use 'slight' advisedly; the majority of mares of all breeds hold to their services, and foal easily and without complications. It is important that your first two mares should be the best you can afford; in pedigree, conformation and temperament. Don't forget temperament. Apart from the fact that you want your foals to be nice-tempered, you want mares that are friendly and easy to handle, because when you start your stud you will probably be working on your own. This is one of the reasons I suggest you buy two mares; anyone can manage two, and later their foals, on their own. Another reason is that horses like company; two mares are really less trouble than one, certainly two foals are. While they are with their dams they play together, which is good for them and exercises them; when weaning time comes they have each other for company, as have the mares. It is always more of a problem to wean a 'single' than two or more foals. Also, after weaning, two foals can share a box when they come in at night during their first winter.

If you breed good stock, and get good prices if you sell, you can, of course, expand and employ help. But if you start with two first-class foundation mares, and they breed you their fair share of fillies, you need never buy any more females unless you see one you desperately want. It is part of the fun and point of a stud, to found a family, based on the female progeny, and their progeny, of your original mare, or mares. To do this is fascinating; you must study pedigrees carefully, deciding when to outcross that is, to use a stallion with no, or few, blood lines similar to those already in your stock, and when you can go back to the line of a stallion who has already given you good foals – even to that stallion himself.

Until you have been going for some time don't be tempted to keep your colt foals entire. Have them gelded either very young or when they are about a year old; your vet will advise you which is best. On the whole, people tend to keep far too many colts uncut; relatively few stallions are necessary for the maintenance of any breed, and those should be of the very best. Until you have made a name for your stud and your line of breeding no one will fall over themselves to buy a colt of yours for use. Good geldings are always saleable, especially if you can afford to keep yours until they are old enough to be broken.

Moreover, colt foals are more precocious than you may think! They are quite capable of getting mares into foal when they are a year old; some even younger. If you don't geld yours, you will have the bother and expense of separate paddocks for them. Gelded, your male and female young stock can run out safely together. There is a legal aspect to this, too. Anyone keeping a colt entire beyond two years must, by law, have him licensed. This costs money.

Keeping a Stallion

If as time goes on you decide to stand a stallion of your own, you will need some extra amenities, because it will only pay you to keep a stallion if you accept visiting mares, who should be kept separate from your own. So you will probably have to do some more fencing. You may like to let your stallion run out with his mares, but as not all mares will come into season at the same time, nor could he serve them all if they did, this will mean careful and constant observation on your part. You will not only have to check on which mares are in season and put them in with him, but you must note on what dates he serves which ones, for owners will want to know this. Even if he does run out with his mares you will probably get some owners who don't want to leave their mares, and who bring them to be served in hand. So you must have somewhere you can use as a covering yard. And even if the stallion does spend a lot of his time outdoors, he still needs a large, roomy box of his own, into which you can take him for feeding, grooming, preparing for shows, and where he can spend the winter nights. Certainly, try to treat him as normally as you would treat any other horse. Ride him if he is broken; if he is not, and he is not too old, break him, so that in winter he can get his exercise under saddle. But remember, he is a stallion. Fences round the fields he uses should be high enough to stop him enthusiastically jumping over them to visit some attractive mare you hadn't noticed was in season; and the lower half-door of his box should be sturdy, with two strong bolts, top and bottom. I would say that you cannot run a stallion without the help of someone as experienced as yourself. You can, of course, train students for stud work if you have taken your NPS Diploma.

Registration

To go back for a moment to the dear old mare we talked about at the beginning. You may actually own such an animal; perhaps she has been your favourite hunter, or you have ridden competitively on her; or she may even be the pony you learnt to ride on, or have had special fun with. There is no reason why you should not use her as your foundation mare, if you think she will breed a good foal. But do be particular about the stallion you choose for her. If she has no 'papers', isn't registered as being of any particular breed I would send her, to an Arab, if there's a good one in your district. The reason for this is that her progeny can then be registered in the Part-Bred Arab Stud Book and if you are starting a stud you must produce stock that can be registered as *something*. Or you could send her to a Welsh Pony or Cob stallion, as the Welsh Pony and Cob Society also run a Part-Bred register. Certain other Breed Societies run Part-Bred registers; before doing any kind of cross-breeding always find out from the Society with which the stallion is registered, whether or not it does so. And never forget to register your own young stock, male and female, but particularly female.

Most studs, in fact all commercial ones, have prefixes or suffixes which they attach to the registered names of all the animals they breed. When you have thought of yours you must register it with your particular Breed Society.

You can, however, use the same prefix or suffix for all your animals, of whatever breed.

The advantage of a stud is that provided you don't let it get too big and take up too much of your time you can carry on with it when you marry, if your husband lives and works in the country; or, conversely, if you are a man and you marry someone who likes country life. As your children become old enough, they will be a help, specially if you are breeding ponies; moreover when they grow up and marry and leave home, you won't be left wondering what to do with your middle age, as so many people are. On the contrary, having fewer responsibilities, you will probably expand your stud and do even more.

Working on Your Own

There are in the horse world quite a few ways in which you can make a living on your own without a great deal of initial expenditure, and which you can continue with, if and when you marry. To me, it always seems a pity that so many girls and young women train for, and pass, their Instructor's or their Stud examinations, and then, the moment they marry, stop using their qualifications. Obviously, this must happen sometimes, but it need not happen nearly so often as it does. There are interesting and lucrative sidelines you can work from your home. Nowadays, when normal household chores are so simplified by endless domestic appliances, there really is no reason to think that you have to give up your profession entirely when you marry.

Show-Jumping

Before we go into those, however, I am sure some of you are wondering why I haven't yet said anything about the profession of show-jumping, now that it is officially recognized that the sport can also be a full-time profession. My answer to that, and to all of you who have the idea that all you need to hit the high spots and the big money is a good horse and talent, is that the odds against any particular individual actually earning their living at the game are very long indeed. It is a far more specialized, and initially expensive, sport or profession than you have probably realized. Of course, if your parents are well off and can afford to buy you good horses and see that you have first-class coaching, you may well get to the top. Also, if you are talented, have the gift of being able to pick out young horses with potential, buy them cheap and make them yourself, you may well be the type to succeed. But where is the money going to come from to buy even your reasonably priced youngsters, and to keep them (and you) while you bring them on?

If you are absolutely determined to jump, your best bet is probably to set yourself up in a 'bread and butter' business, a riding, hacking or livery stable, and, if you have the right horse and enough help to look after things while you are away, jump at as many shows as you can and see how you make out. Or go to work for a riding or training establishment where the owner is a jumping enthusiast, and who, if you are really good, will encourage you and let you jump good horses. With a bit of luck, you may catch a sponsor's eye. But always remember that though the prize money nowadays is high, so is the cost of keeping and travelling top-class horses. Although the life may appear glamorous to the onlooker – all that jumping in lighted arenas in front of huge crowds (and television cameras), and being presented with silver trophies or Volkswagens or Saddles of Honour by the Queen or Sir Mike Ansell – for every rider who gets into that kind of limelight the number of those who do not, is legion.

Event Horse Training

'Eventing' is an amateur sport but can indirectly be of great benefit to you professionally. If you set up a riding establishment of any kind, sooner or later you are bound to want to try to train an event horse, and produce it yourself, or let one of your best pupils do so. If the horse performs reasonably well this will add to the reputation of your establishment. Similarly, if you are running a stud and happen to breed a good event horse, which you either produce yourself or which is known to be of your breeding, this will be an excellent advertisement for your stud. Here, incidentally, is one of those sidelines which could continue to be an outlet for your talents when you marry. If you get a name for training event horses it will be perfectly possible for you, if you live in the country, to take one or two horses, or riders with their own horses, for periods of concentrated schooling and coaching.

Another similar sideline, if you live in the country after marriage and have been specially interested in breaking and making, is to take young horses or ponies in to handle, break and school on. You won't need a lot of facilities: a field, a loose box (two if possible), a large enough piece of flat ground to make a lungeing and working arena, lungeing equipment and an outhouse in which to store feeding stuffs. I would take them in spring, summer and early autumn only; working young horses in winter without a covered school can be unpleasant weather-wise, besides, you want a rest some time. And I would never take in more than two at any one time; if you are on your own, two is enough to cope with. Working with young horses is not only a very satisfactory occupation but a very necessary one. As I have already said, far too few people with the proper skill and knowledge concentrate on it. If you decide to break, make and school young horses at home you will be surprised by the number of replies you get if you put an advertisement in your local paper. But remember to work out your charges in advance; be sure they not only cover the keep of the young horse but also recompense you adequately for your own time. This can be a lucrative addition to the family income.

Freelance Teaching

If you are a particularly gifted and dedicated teacher, and have your BHS Instructor's exam, perhaps you are even a Fellow of the Society, you can work as a freelance instructor. If you are married you can have pupils come with their horses to your home, or you can take courses and classes in the neighbourhood. If you are single you can travel all over the country. What's more, there is no age limit. Provided you remain active enough to be able, if you wish, to get on to other people's horses to demonstrate or to 'sort them out', you can go on instructing when you are a grandmother. First-class freelance instructors who are willing to travel and take courses anywhere can do an enormous amount of good, because their teaching will reach many more people than would ever be able to transport themselves and their horses long distances for concentrated instruction. Riding Clubs, Pony Clubs and dedicated individuals from John o' Groats to Land's End are all potential clients. This is a most interesting way of earning a living; you not only see a lot of the country, you meet many people and make many friends. It can also be tiring. Probably the least exhausting way of coping with a lot of travelling is to have some sort of motorized living accommodation and drive yourself about. People will always offer to put you up, but at the end of a day's teaching, you may find it more restful to retire into the privacy of your caravanette than to spend the evening in horsey conversation.

Obviously before you decide to freelance you should

have made a certain reputation for yourself as a teacher; perhaps as Chief Instructor at a good school, or a school of your own, or as the trainer of a number of successful competitive pupils. You could then ask the British Horse Society to put you on to their list of official 'Visiting Instructors', which is sent to all riding clubs, and ask the Pony Club to do the same. Although the majority of regular Pony Club instructors are voluntary, most clubs are glad to pay fees to professionals for special help, perhaps with their annual summer camps or their Inter-Branch teams.

In the last few years, there has been a great revival of interest in side-saddle riding. If this appeals to you, it might be worth your while some time during your career to take a side-saddle course. It would certainly extend your scope as an Instructor. The British Horse Society would be able to give you the names of people qualified to teach side-saddle.

Today many people combine running a riding school or livery yard with running a shop. Some are very comprehensive, carrying a varied stock of everything even remotely connected with horses and riding, others specialize in tack and stable equipment. If you have the premises and the business ability, or a husband, or wife, with the latter, there is no reason why you shouldn't run such a shop from your home even without an attendant riding school. It could be a good commercial proposition.

And last, if you have imagination and the gift of words you can write about horses. Not necessarily anything highly technical or knowledgeable; stories for children, perhaps, or for your own children. You will find that there is plenty to write about, once you start, and, who knows, one day your stories may find their way into print.

9   Summing Up

The rewards of a career with horses. Producing a successful pupil; a good horse; perhaps competing successfully. The joy of riding itself – which is one of the few outdoor activities one can continue to do into old age. (Mrs Johnstone, represented her country in the Olympics at seventy!) The satisfaction of being able to help others to a greater understanding of horses and enlarge their knowledge of horse management.

In this present age many of us have to live in such artificial surroundings that we can easily forget that, as human beings, we are essentially part of a living, animate world. Although we humans may be special because our brains can think, reason and invent all sorts of useful and terrifying things; in fact, we are only one of the myriad species of living organisms sharing the world with us.

It seems to me that anything, whether a job or a hobby, that can take us occasionally out of the world of the machine into the world of nature, must be beneficial. For instance, I am sure that one of the reasons why in recent years so many people have taken up riding and horse-owning is because they feel they must somehow compensate themselves for the sameness of their ordinary lives; the drabness of doing the same things day after day, at work or at leisure.

Changing Times

Time is curious, and would seem to be a wheel rather than a straight line. 'The whirligig of time', Shakespeare calls it, and it certainly does 'have its revenges'. In the past almost everyone, from king to costermonger, kept horses, even in cities, and rode or drove because they had to. It was the motor car, when it first arrived which was the escape: the horse, the routine. Now, having progressed from the motor car to the moon, it is the machine in all its forms from which, if we are to retain our sanity and our humanity, we must now and then escape.

One of the principal rewards, therefore, of a career with horses, or with any animal, is that it lets us earn our livelihoods at work which is mainly out of doors. Of course, there is routine attached to it, as there is to work of any kind. However it is routine not simply for its own sake, but for that of the animals who depend on us. Besides, the care of horses, their grooming, feeding and exercising, can never be entirely routine. Horses are individuals. One that was lazy yesterday may feel on top of the world today and have a shot at bucking you off. Another may decide not to eat. Why? Another may cast a shoe, or catch a cold, or become inexplicably lame, or get colic. Moreover, working stable routine, it is impossible not to become aware of the year's changing seasons: the frosty, starry nights of winter – rugs, blankets, clipped-out horses; the lightening, lengthening days of spring – birdsong, trees and flowers in bud, winter coats shedding, summer ones showing through the clip; the haze of summer – bees, hay-making, trees and hedges in heavy leaf, glossy show-coats or roughed-off hunters in lush meadows; the swing towards harvest – stubble fields, gold leaves, lighted windows riding home at dusk, time to clip out again before winter, and another cycle of the year begins. Unless man's brain manages to destroy this earth on which we live, working with horses we know that 'while the earth remaineth, seedtime and harvest, cold and heat and summer and winter and night and day shall not cease', which is a comforting and stabilizing knowledge, even if we never formulate it.

The Rewards

But now to more particular and individual rewards. If you are a teacher your greatest reward will be the success of some really talented pupil whom you have discovered and trained. This won't happen as often as you might think. Most of your teaching life will be spent making the best of mediocre, if enthusiastic, material. And though the brilliant teacher can work apparent miracles with any pupil who is sufficiently dedicated, to be presented with a genuine talent, and be given the chance of helping it to develop its full potential, is a gift from the gods indeed. If in the fulness of time your discovery hits the headlines and the TV cameras, while naturally it will add to your reputation, more importantly, it will give you the same sense of fulfilment creative artists know when they finish their painting or their poem or their symphony.

However, let me hasten to add, you will also get great satisfaction from the improvement of your more ordinary pupils, some of whom may reward you by becoming very much better than you ever thought possible. No one can make a silk purse out of a sow's ear; but sows' ears can make perfectly respectable leather ones!

In breeding, the reward for producing a really top-class animal may come to you quite quickly; it may take years to achieve or it may never come at all, because however scientifically we go about it in breeding there is always an element of chance. If you do happen to breed an animal that becomes a Supreme Champion, or an international event horse, or show-jumper, try to remember that although your choice of sire and dam and your good care of the youngster have combined to produce the paragon, the actual success belongs to the animal. I say this because you do come across people in the showing world who tend to behave as though it were they, and not their horses, who had won the rosettes decorating their tack rooms, or the cups on their sideboards. Of course the horses could not have won without them, and it is very true that a good animal, well produced in the ring, will often beat a better one that is badly shown. Nevertheless, great success always rests ultimately with the horse. You can breed what in conformation may be the almost perfect horse or pony; if it hasn't got that indefinable something that in humans we call 'star quality', the very top will always elude it.

Showing does tend to bring out some not-so-attractive human characteristics if you let yourself become too deadly earnest about it. Parents can be the worst offenders by being so intent on their children winning that the children become almost frightened not to, especially if they have been bought ponies that are far too expensive just to have fun with. Then again, if the children are good and win fairly consistently, it's difficult for them not to get a bit big-headed towards children whose parents aren't so well-off and can't buy such expensive animals. All of which must tend to spoil children's enjoyment of riding, which is a pity. The adult characteristic most often brought out by showing, in both males and females, is the really rather funny one of cattiness! Outsiders at the ringside happening to overhear one exhibitor talking about other exhibitors' animals, might quite easily be led to believe there was only one pony is the class that actually had a head, a tail and four sound legs!

Judging

Showing, however, can be enjoyable and instructive for all of us, provided we don't lose our sense of values, and it is a must, for breeders. If you do breed and show fairly successfully one of the rewards which may come your way will be that you may be asked to judge. Probably you will first be asked to go on the judges' panel of your particular breed; or, at smaller shows, you may

G

be plunged into judging not only your breed but others as well. Maybe you don't think this is a reward, but it is. Judges are expected to be people of impartiality and integrity, so, if you are ever asked, judge and be damned. And be prepared, on the day, to stand by your own opinion.

You should, however, make a few preparations. If you are judging your own breed, you will know exactly what you are looking for. If others as well, you must mug up on the special characteristics of each, for although your eye should enable you to tell the good from the less good of any breed, each has certain particularities of conformation, markings, perhaps of colouring, to which all the animals in front of you should more or less conform. It is also a good idea to make up your mind about what you consider to be the more permissible *faults*. No horse or pony is perfect; it is the one with the fewest faults of conformation and of action that should win. It is important to remember this, because sometimes a very eye-catching animal will come into the ring and you can't help but pull it in first, only to discover when you look at each animal individually that there are others, less showy, that are in fact better. So never be afraid to alter your original placings, and don't be put off by glares from whoever is leading, or riding, the animal you have displaced. Probably, like many judges, you will have a favourite good point, which, all other things being equal between two animals, will swing the balance one way or the other; maybe a specially good head, or hind leg, or shoulder, or depth of girth. Remember, however, that no really good horse can have faulty *action*.

Judging is fascinating, but it isn't easy, and you will make it more difficult for yourself if you let your eyes stray from the animals to the people leading or riding them. It won't help you to say to yourself: 'That's so-and-so, theirs are always good, I better put them up.' For all you know, so-and-so may have been asked to show for someone else that day; even if they are showing one of their own that happened to win the week before that's no reason for you to place it anywhere other than where *you* think it should be. Judges, obviously, must not see the list of exhibitors' names beforehand, nor must they ask chatty questions in the ring; the only one you may legitimately ask is the age of the animal you are looking at.

Professionalism

Another of the rewards of working professionally with horses is that the unknowledgeable will accept help and advice from us because we are professionals. We can explain to them why they should not ride their two-year-olds, nor buy yearlings for their children; why it is not really kind to turn their old horse out into a unsheltered paddock because they love him too much to have him put down, and many other basic things. It also gives us the authority, when necessary, to try to right the worst equine wrongs we may come across, and there are still quite a lot of these. In spite of the Riding Establishments Act, wild-cat riding schools and holiday and trekking centres do exist; moreover, conditions in all the Licensed ones are not always what they should be. For the sake of the animals, I think you should accept the responsibility that being trained and qualified imposes on you, and report instances of bad conditions and bad management. First, you should find out if the establishment has, in fact, a Licence. If it has, report to the Authority concerned, and to the Riding Establishments Act Committee of the British Horse Society. If it hasn't, report to the local Authority that it exists, and should be inspected. There are always people who won't take any of these steps for fear of becoming personally unpopular; a selfish attitude for anyone to take who is truly interested in the welfare of horses.

If you run a riding school or a stud one of the pleasant, and perhaps surprising, discoveries you will make is the number of children, both boys and girls, who not only want to ride, but to learn all about horses and ponies. If you let them come to your stable or stud at weekends, and take the trouble to teach them, they will often turn out to be better and more dedicated workers than many grown-ups. Children, incidentally, are very good with foals, who seem to find them easier to accept than adults, probably because they're so much smaller. Foals will often let children handle them before they will accept us, and very seldom try the usual little foal naughtinesses on them.

Another pleasant discovery is the genuine camaraderie that exists between all who are seriously interested in the art of good riding; the endless and fascinating discussions you can have on this endlessly fascinating subject. These discussions will broaden your outlook, give you new ideas, and encourage you to go on always trying to improve yourself.

Most interesting, however, will be the discoveries you will make about horses themselves. You will discover that horses, given the chance, can be companions; not just when you are riding them, but when they are being themselves, in their fields or boxes. They do recognize their owners, or those who habitually care for them, and some, if you repeat it often enough, can learn to recognize their names. Opinions differ as to whether or not horses have much intelligence; what is certain, however, is that the more you handle any particular horse, the more his intelligence will develop. This incidentally is exactly the same with dogs; an unhandled, untrained dog will appear to be much more stupid than a trained one. You will discover that horses are individuals, and that mares and geldings have distinctly different characters. Some people prefer one, some the other. I have always found that mares tend to be more one man (or woman) animals than geldings;

that may be simply because I have had a specially good understanding with several mares. You will discover that whether or not horses have much intelligence, they have very long memories. They remember for as long as the proverbial elephant, and if they get the chance, can take their revenge on someone who has been deliberately unkind to them long after you may think they have forgotten. Equally, because they are very sensitive to sound they will respond with confidence to a familiar voice even if they haven't heard it for years. They remember places well, though why we should be surprised that animals do this I can't imagine. And some, especially ponies, can be quite extraordinarily clever at annoying tricks like undoing knots, unlatching gates, opening food bins, even turning on taps, and, of course, at knowing which riders or handlers they must respect and of which they can take advantage. Many horses, if you have handled them a lot, can even be good patients when they are sick, seeming to connect what you are doing to them with feeling better or more comfortable, whereas those without confidence in humans can fuss and be a nuisance.

Soldiering On

Undoubtedly, though, the greatest reward of a career with horses is that it is one from which you will not have to retire when you are sixty or sixty-five. Nor will you feel like doing so, because riding will have kept you at least ten years younger than your actual age. In body because you will stay supple, muscled and exercised; and in mind because the pleasure that riding and your horses give you is a continual refreshment and challenge.

When she was seventy Mrs Lorna Johnstone represented her country in the Olympic Games of 1972, where she was not only the most successful member of the British Dressage team, but the most successful British rider ever to have competed in Olympic Dressage. Nor has she been content to sit back and rest upon the laurels of that remarkable achievement. In her eighth decade she has bought a new horse and is training it.

So you see, a career with horses, especially one which involves riding, not only offers you a way of life but a way you can follow, and continue to learn about, all your life.

Appendix:
Some Books of
General Interest

Books, instructional and informative and of general interest.

The first person to have formulated a theory of practical horsemanship was the Greek writer Xenophon, who lived some 400 years BC, and whose *Art of Horsemanship* survives as a classic to this day (in translation by Professor Morgan). Since then, literally countless books have been written, not only about every aspect of equestrianism, but about every aspect of horse-keeping and horse management. No one can read them all, nor can I give you a list of them all, only of those which I personally have found to be of particular interest and use, and those which the British Horse Society recommends to be read by examination candidates.

For everyone interested in books about horses, J. A. Allen and Co. Ltd, 1 Lower Grosvenor Place, Buckingham Palace Road, London SW1 0EL, are the booksellers to contact. If you cannot go to them, they will send you their catalogues regularly. These in themselves make fascinating reading, and if you are a book addict, will encourage you to add to your library.

First for the books which BHS examination candidates must read because the principles laid down in them are those to which the examiners will expect you to confirm on exam day. All are published by the British Horse Society, with the exception of the two veterinary ones, which can, however, be obtained from the Society.

EXAMINATION BOOKS

The Manual of Horsemanship (British Horse Society Publication).

The Instructor's Handbook (British Horse Society Publication).

Keeping a Pony at Grass (British Horse Society Publication).

Training the Young Pony (British Horse Society Publication).

First Aid Hints for Horse Owners, Lt-Col. W. E. Lyon (Collins). This is a remarkably clear, easy to follow book for the layman, whether or not taking an exam.

Know Your Horse, Lt-Col. W. S. Codrington, MRCVS (J. A. Allen & Co. Ltd). Another book which all horse-owners would find invaluable.

INSTRUCTIONAL AND INFORMATIVE BOOKS ON RIDING

Learning to Ride and Pony Care, W. J. W. Froud (Hamlyn). This is for the fairly young, but anyone teaching the young would find it immensely useful. It is a well-produced book, beautifully illustrated.

Riding, Mrs V. D. S. Williams (published for the British Horse Society by Educational Productions Ltd). Particularly good diagrams and illustrations; can supplement *The Manual of Horsemanship*.

Riding For All, R. S. Summerhayes.* An excellent book, with the advantage that it is available in paperback.

Equitation, Henry Wynmalen (J. A. Allen & Co. Ltd).

Dressage, Henry Wynmalen (J. A. Allen & Co. Ltd). Both invaluable for the dedicated rider.

Jumping : Learning and Teaching, Jean Frossard (Pelham Books). Clear, concise, excellent photographs.

Teach Your Horse to Jump, W. J. W. Froud (Thomas Nelson & Sons Ltd). The best book I have come across on teaching the horse, rather than the rider; an aspect of the jumping game not always taken seriously enough.

Riding Logic, Wilhelm Müseler (Eyre Methuen). A fairly advanced book, the translation from the German sometimes a little involved but a book from which the serious rider can learn a lot.

The Event Horse, Sheila Willcox (Pelham Books). Comprehensive on the training and conditioning of the event horse.

Stable Management and Exercise, Capt. M. Horace Hayes (Stanley Paul). A classic, as are all the books Captain Hayes has written and which are now reprinted. If you can lay your hands on any, buy them!

BOOKS OF SPECIAL INTEREST TO BREEDERS AND STUD OWNERS

Horses and Riding, E. Skelton (Stanley Paul). This book is officially recommended by the National Pony Society to be read by candidates for its Stud examinations.

Mares, Foals and Foaling, Friedrich Andrist (J. A. Allen & Co. Ltd). A 'must' for the owner-breeder; a short, concise, clearly illustrated explanation of the process of foaling, with advice on the care of brood mares, foals and weanlings.

Rearing a Foal, Jane Howell (Thomas Nelson & Sons Ltd). Again, a 'must' for the breeder just starting, or the owner of a single mare and foal.

The Way of a Horse, Marguerite de Beaumont (J. A.

Allen & Co. Ltd). Both informative on stud management and highly enjoyable, easy reading.

Stallions: Their Management and Handling, Neil Dougall (J. A. Allen & Co. Ltd). Clear, comprehensive and exactly what it says it is.

From Paddock to Saddle, E. Hartley Edwards (Thomas Nelson & Sons Ltd). An admirable book on the training of the young horse, from handling and leading through lungeing, backing and schooling, to the final production of the well-mannered riding horse. Particularly lucid explanation, with diagrams, of how to lunge correctly and why one lunges.

Horse Breeding and Stud Management, Henry Wynmalen (J. A. Allen & Co. Ltd). All Wynmalen's books are worth having, well written, easy to read and communicating the author's dedication to his subject and his horses.

Ringcraft, E. Skelton (Thomas Nelson & Sons Ltd).

Handbook of Showing, Glenda Spooner (Museum Press). Both these books are helpful and include a lot of technical advice on showing.

Horse Psychology, Dr Moyra Williams (Methuen). This is an unusual book which I find deeply interesting and I think most people in close and everyday contact with horses would find it equally so. Dr Williams has written other books which are also highly interesting.

Talking of Horses, Monica Dickens (Heinemann). Another unusual book by the well-known novelist which gives new insights into the characters and temperaments of horses.

The Foals of Epoha, Daphne Machin Goodall and Anthony Dent (Galley Press Ltd). A history of the British native pony breeds. A fascinating reference book for breeders of Mountain and Moorlands.

BOOKS ON NATIONAL HUNT RACING

The Sport of Queens, Dick Francis (Michael Joseph).

Mr Grand National, David Hedges (Pelham Books Ltd). The biography of Fred Winter, who as a jockey made quite a speciality of winning Grand Nationals and is continuing to do so as a trainer.

Arkle, Ivor Herbert (Pelham Books Ltd). The story of a great steeplechaser.

Golden Miller, Gregory Blaxland (Constable & Co. Ltd). The story of Arkle's most famous predecessor.

Red Rum, Ivor Herbert (William Luscombe). The story of his most famous successor.

Right Royal, John Masefield.* This is an epic poem about a particular steeplechase; incredibly vivid and exciting. It is, of course, in Masefield's Collected Poems, but has also been published separately with illustrations. Not many people know it, but I assure you it is as thrilling, and easy to read, as any novel.

There are a great many more books on this subject and so many on flat-racing that it would be invidious to pick out any. Besides, flat-racing enthusiasts are usually born and not made, and if any read this book, will already have their individual favourites. Incidentally, don't forget Dick Francis's thrillers; all about racing or jumping, and all accurate in detail, nor are the adventures of their various heroes too far-fetched.

There are also many books on hunting. Three classics which you may not know, however, and which you would enjoy are:

Memoirs of a Fox-hunting Man, Siegfried Sassoon (Faber & Faber Ltd).

Experiences of an Irish RM, E. O. E. Somerville and Martin Ross (Faber & Faber Ltd).

Further Experiences of an Irish RM, E. O. E. Somerville and Martin Ross (Faber & Faber Ltd). Can be re-read again and again; gloriously funny in parts.

If you are particularly interested in hounds:
The Book of the Foxhound, Daphne Moore (J. A. Allen & Co. Ltd). The work of today's acknowledged expert.

Finally, five books which give me continual pleasure:
Tschiffely's Ride, A. P. Tschiffely.* This is the story of an amazing endurance ride from Buenos Aires to Washington DC by the author and two Criollo horses, Mancha and Gato. My copy is practically falling to pieces by now.
Two Middle-aged Ladies in Andalusia, Penelope Chetwode (John Murray Ltd). Enchanting. The two ladies are the author and her mare who explore Andalusia together.
My Dancing White Horses, Alois Podhajsky (George G. Harrap & Co. Ltd).
My Horses, My Teachers, Alois Podhajsky (George G. Harrap & Co. Ltd). Colonel Podhajsky was for many years principal of the Spanish Riding School, Vienna. Beautifully illustrated books, emanating the author's dedication to his school, his art and his horses.
The Trainers, Ann Martin (Stanley Paul). Short biographies, profiles, of some of today's best-known trainers of all disciplines; eventing, dressage, show-jumping, and showing. Particularly interesting sidelights on the different methods of five of the most successful Horse Trials trainers: Captain Goldman, Bertie Hill, Alison Oliver, Lars Sederholm and Dick Stilwell.

* Out of print and therefore no longer available. Try your local public library.

Index